How to Manage the Classroom

The Complete Guide

By Mike Gershon

Text Copyright © 2015 Mike Gershon

All Rights Reserved

Series Introduction

The 'How to...' series developed out of Mike's desire to share great classroom practice with teachers around the world. He wanted to put together a collection of books which would help professionals no matter what age group or subject they were teaching.

Each volume focuses on a different element of classroom practice and each is overflowing with brilliant, practical strategies, techniques and activities – all of which are clearly explained and ready-to-use. In most cases, the ideas can be applied immediately, helping teachers not only to teach better but to save time as well.

All of the books have been designed to help teachers. Each one goes out of its way to make educators' lives easier and their lessons even more engaging, inspiring and successful then they already are.

In addition, the whole series is written from the perspective of a working teacher. It takes account of the realities of the classroom, blending theoretical insight with a consistently practical focus.

The 'How to...' series is great teaching made easy.

Author Introduction

Mike Gershon is a teacher, trainer and writer. He is the author of over twenty books on teaching, learning and education, including a number of bestsellers, as well as the co-author of four others. Mike's online resources have been viewed and downloaded more than 2.8 million times by teachers in over 180 countries and territories. He writes regularly for the Times Educational Supplement and has created over 40 guides to different areas of teaching and learning as well as two online courses covering outstanding teaching and growth mindsets. Find out more, get in touch and download free resources at www.mikegershon.com

Training and Consultancy

Mike is an expert trainer whose sessions have received acclaim from teachers across England. Recent bookings include:

- *Growth Mindsets: Theory and Practice*

- *AFL Unlocked: Using Feedback and Marking to Raise Achievement*

- *Success in Linear Assessment: Strategies to Support Learners*

Mike also works as a consultant, advising on teaching and learning and creating bespoke materials for schools. Recent work includes:

- *Improving Literacy and Academic Language*

- *Growth Mindset Assemblies and Pastoral Support Materials*

If you would like speak to Mike about the services he can offer your school, please get in touch by email: mike@mikegershon.com

Acknowledgements

As ever I must thank all the fantastic colleagues and students I have worked with over the years, first while training at the Institute of Education, Central Foundation Girls' School and Nower Hill High School and subsequently while working at Pimlico Academy and King Edward VI School in Bury St Edmunds. Thanks especially to Kurt and Cathy from Pimlico, whose consummate skill in managing behaviour taught me a huge amount when I first started out in the classroom.

Other Works from the Same Author

Available to buy now on Amazon:

How to use Differentiation in the Classroom: The Complete Guide

How to use Assessment for Learning in the Classroom: The Complete Guide

How to use Questioning in the Classroom: The Complete Guide

How to use Discussion in the Classroom: The Complete Guide

How to Teach EAL Students in the Classroom: The Complete Guide

How to be an Outstanding Trainee Teacher: The Complete Guide

How to use Bloom's Taxonomy in the Classroom: The Complete Guide

How to Manage Behaviour in the Classroom: The Complete Guide

More Secondary Starters and Plenaries

Secondary Starters and Plenaries: History

Teach Now! History: Becoming a Great History Teacher

The Growth Mindset Pocketbook (with Professor Barry Hymer)

How to be Outstanding in the Classroom: Raising achievement, securing progress and making learning happen

Also available to buy now on Amazon, the entire 'Quick 50' Series:

50 Quick and Brilliant Teaching Ideas

50 Quick and Brilliant Teaching Techniques

50 Quick and Brilliant Teaching Games

50 Quick and Easy Lesson Activities

50 Quick Ways to Help Your Students Secure A and B Grades at GCSE

50 Quick Ways to Help Your Students Think, Learn, and Use Their Brains Brilliantly

50 Quick Ways to Motivate and Engage Your Students

50 Quick Ways to Outstanding Teaching

50 Quick Ways to Perfect Behaviour Management

50 Quick Ways to Outstanding Group Work

50 Quick and Easy Ways to Prepare for Ofsted

50 Quick and Easy Ways Leaders can Prepare for Ofsted

50 Quick and Brilliant Ideas for English Teaching (with Lizi Summers)

50 Quick and Easy Ways to Build Resilience through English Teaching (with Lizi Summers)

50 Quick and Easy Ways to Outstanding English Teaching (with Lizi Summers)

Table of Contents

Introduction 11
Chapter One – What is Behaviour? 15
Chapter Two – Norms, Values, Roles and Status 33
Chapter Three – Rules, Boundaries and Consistency 49
Chapter Four – Planning for Learning 65
Chapter Five – Using Praise 83
Chapter Six – Eliminating Low-Level Disruption 97
Chapter Seven – Creating Engagement 113
Chapter Eight – Building Rapport 129
Chapter Nine – Common Problems and Scenarios 145
Chapter Ten – Collected Chapter Summaries 159
Conclusion 165
Select Bibliography 167

Introduction

Hello and welcome to 'How to Manage Behaviour in the Classroom: The Complete Guide.' This book gives you all the practical strategies, tried-and-tested tips, useful techniques and real-world advice you need to create a focussed, positive learning environment, every time you teach.

It's a book based on experience and a book rooted in the reality of classroom life. There are no magic bullets and no golden wands to wave. But everything from here on out will help you to foster a classroom culture which allows you to raise achievement, maximise progress and provide students with the kind of productive, stimulating experiences they will remember, value, and learn from.

Everything to come rests on a simple proposition: children and young adults are learning, we are teaching them. This dictum extends beyond the formal curriculum and into the world of morals, manners and behaviour – just as it has done for many years previous.

Part of our job as teachers is to help students understand what is acceptable and what is not, how to behave in certain situations, what the unwritten rules of society amount to, and how to rise up to meet and exceed the high expectations with which others present us.

Thinking about behaviour in this way – as something students are learning – helps us to focus what we are best at – teaching – on that part of the job we might like the least, or find the most difficult to deal with.

You are a good teacher, I'm sure of it. You know how to plan learning, open up ideas, and develop understanding. You also know how to stimulate students' curiosity and challenge them to think more deeply. You can use these skills – skills you already possess – to manage behaviour effectively; even brilliantly.

Seeing behaviour management as an extension of the wider teaching in which we engage does not mean denying the responsibility pupils have to behave well, or the necessity of applying sanctions if they break the rules. But it does mean seeing even these things as part of students' learning. In childhood and the teenage years, boundaries are pushed. This is an extension of the trial and error and uninhibited play which form the cornerstone of much of our development. We are trying to ascertain, whether knowingly or not, how we may interact with the world around us.

Thinking about behaviour in this way has an important consequence.

If we accept that students are learning about behaviour then we accept that their behaviour can be changed. As such, we avoid labels and speak always about the behaviour, never the child. This means we don't say things like 'you're a troublemaker' but instead say things like 'you're behaviour is causing trouble and I would like you to make a different choice.' The first formulation labels the child as fixed and unchanging; the second formulation labels the behaviour and indicates that change is possible.

It is easy to see why the latter option is always to be preferred.

With those thoughts at the front of our minds, let me provide a brief overview of what you can expect in the chapters which follow.

Chapter One does the groundwork for us, examining what behaviour is, where it comes from and how we might look at it critically in the context of the classroom. Chapter Two builds on this by providing a sociological analysis of behaviour in the classroom and an explanation of how we can think effectively about, and begin to shape, the kind of learning environment we want.

Chapter Three looks at rules, boundaries and consistency, providing guidance on how to formulate and apply the first two before explaining why the third one is so important. Then, in Chapter Four, we look at practical strategies we can use to ensure our planning is as effective as possible in facilitating excellent behaviour.

Chapter Five turns our attention to that most vital of behaviour management tools: praise. Then, in Chapter Six, we look at one of the major bug-bears for many teachers when it comes to behaviour, how to eliminate low-level disruption.

Chapters Seven and Eight sit as a pair, the first examining how we can build rapport and the second looking at strategies for creating engagement. Chapter Nine then examines a series of common behaviour problems and scenarios, offering three practical solutions for each situation.

All of these chapters are concluded with a short bullet-point summary of the key aims. I have collected all of these together in Chapter Ten to give you an easy point of reference, to which you can turn whenever you need help but are short on time.

So there you have it: our path has been staked out and all that remains is for me to invite you to walk along it. I hope you find the journey informative, useful and interesting. But, most of all, I hope it gives you everything you need to establish a superb environment for learning every time you teach.

Chapter One – What is Behaviour?

We begin, as we must, by trying to define what we actually mean by behaviour. To do so will give us a clearer sense of what we are seeking to manage whenever we find ourselves faced with a roomful of students. Without a sound basis for defining behaviour, we risk operating from a position of uncertainty. This makes it harder for us to think critically about the behaviour in our classrooms, to make good decisions about how to manage it, and to reflect with accuracy on the results of our efforts.

It is easy to dismiss such an approach. Behaviour, after all, is something we know well and with which we are familiar. However, if we want to manage behaviour as effectively as possible, we must begin by turning inwards and examining the assumptions on which our present thinking rests. If we ignore this, we ignore the important process of building foundations upon which our endeavours can sit. It may be that our understanding of behaviour turns out to be sound, but it is better to know this for certain than to assume it to be the case.

For these reasons, this chapter will be more theoretical than the remainder of the book. This is necessary to achieve our aim. However, everything we consider will be related back to classroom practice; it will also provide a framework for the extensive practical guidance which follows.

Behaviour in General

The term behaviour refers to the outward actions in which we engage. These actions are the effects of external or internal causes, or a mixture of the two. For example, I may raise my hands because a ball has been kicked towards my face (external cause), I may go to the kitchen because I feel hungry (internal cause) or I may decide to swerve my car to avoid hitting a rabbit which has strayed onto the road (combination of external and internal causes).

From this starting point we can argue that behaviour effected by external causes is a reaction to something in our environment. Behaviour effected by internal causes is a response to something happening within us. And behaviour effected by a combination involves the intermixing of the environment and that which is internal.

In terms of the classroom, we could imagine students looking up involuntarily to see who is knocking at the door as an example of the first type of behaviour. Then we could imagine students disengaging from their work because they feel hungry as an example of the second. And we could see students deciding to work hard because their teacher, with whom they have a strong relationship, has asked them to as an example of the third.

The argument being made is that external and internal causes often lead us to react without conscious thought, whereas a combination of the two nearly always leads to decisions being made about how to act.

Yet, we also know that all of us – especially children and young adults – can behave in ways which, upon reflection, appear unexpected, regrettable or motivated by a conscious decision we are surprised we took.

For example, we might say something in conversation, believing it to be an appropriate point, and then, upon hearing ourselves say it, immediately regret the decision.

From this it can be suggested that even behaviour which is the result of active decision-making on the part of the individual will not necessarily accord with that individual's desires or intentions. Sometimes it will, sometimes it won't. And, in many cases, the reasoning underlying what has happened may be opaque, at first glance, to all concerned.

Most teachers have come across such situations. A student behaves poorly in class, even though they want to do well. When we ask them why they behaved in such a way, they are unable to articulate an answer, despite knowing it was they who made the choice to act.

This throws up an extremely important point about behaviour in general. We learn how to behave within the society and culture in which we are brought up. This does not mean that our behaviour will be identical to others brought up in a similar way, nor does it seek to exclude differences which are the result of biological factors. But it does intimate that coming to understand how to control and direct our own behaviour is a learning process – often a tricky one.

To this end, all children and young adults, throughout their school lives, are learning how to behave as members of a wider society and culture, as well as learning the content of the curriculum. For this reason, it is important to remember that all teachers are teachers of norms and values – of moral instruction in a broad sense – as well as teachers of subjects and topics.

This is why behaviour management is a significant part of every teacher's job. It is not that all students are predisposed to test the will of the teachers with whom they find themselves. Instead, it is that all students are learning about behaviour – what is acceptable and what isn't, what works and what doesn't, what consequences result from certain decisions – throughout the time that we teach them.

The extent of this learning varies considerably from student to student. This reflects the fact that some students go through their entire school career exhibiting what might only be described as excellent behaviour. Whereas others may have a much different time of it, showcasing behaviour that is contrary to what their teachers (and perhaps they) would want.

All of this indicates, though, that behaviour is malleable. If students are learning about how to behave, about the consequences of their actions, and about how to control and direct the decisions they make, then the things we do in the classroom can really make a difference.

And it is this fact which underlies the entirety of this book, as well as your decision to read it.

Behaviour in the Classroom

The classroom is a specific place in any child's life. It is a space about which they have certain preconceptions and towards which they have certain dispositions. On top of this, they have relationships with their peers and their teachers which influence how they view the classroom in which they find themselves.

This demonstrates how any situation in which we find ourselves (and, therefore, in which we will exhibit behaviour) is characterised by both the physical environment and our response to and interaction with that environment.

So, for example, students in our class perceive the walls of the classroom, the desks, the whiteboard, the displays, their fellow students and ourselves. This is the physical environment. But they also perceive all these things through a system of meaning, signs, memories and assumptions, with this being altered and modified to greater or lesser extents by subsequent interactions.

From here we can begin to understand why students may behave completely differently in the same classroom with two different teachers. The environment in which they exhibit their behaviour is not just a physical, external environment. It is also a cognitive landscape. One built upon the concepts, categories, experiences, memories and so forth which students possess and to which more is added every lesson.

To illustrate the impact of the physical environment, consider how you might alter your behaviour if you found yourself in a place where you felt unsafe. To illustrate the impact of our minds, consider how you would think about the place in which you found yourself if you did feel unsafe. And to illustrate the impact of the interactions we have with the physical environment, consider how you might alter your behaviour if someone in this unsafe place greeted you in a friendly, open and welcoming manner.

Contextualising this example leads us to the following:

A student is used to failing at school and being labelled as incapable of making good progress. They enter your classroom and see it as unsafe for them (psychologically) as a result. This leads them to walk in with a mental safety barrier in place designed to protect them from the unpleasant experiences with which they are familiar. This barrier manifests itself in attitude, appearance, and language (all constituents of behaviour).

Instead of meeting the expectations of this student and validating them, we put them to one side and put forward our own expectations. We greet the student warmly, welcome them to our classroom and tell them we are looking forward to working with them in the lesson.

Harking back to the close of our previous section, this helps us to see how we are in a position to shape the behaviour which happens when we teach. By taking control of the situation in which we find ourselves and by asserting a positive sense of what our classroom is – both in physical terms and in terms of the interactions which happen there – we can shape and mould the thoughts students have, as well as the behaviours to which these give rise.

This again reiterates the points that behaviour can be changed, that it is learned, and that the teacher has it within their power to manage this process – whoever they are and whatever their experience.

Of course, it goes without saying that with experience behaviour management tends to become easier, but then this is true of most things. And it does not exclude the possibility of excellent behaviour management from the very start of your career.

So we find ourselves with two key ideas, thus far, on which we are going to build the rest of the book:

i) Behaviour is learned. That is, it is a result, in no small part, of past experience.

ii) Behaviour can be changed through new learning. That is, through new experiences.

These ideas allow us to see our own actions as meaningful. They help us to avoid falling into a situation from where we feel that, no matter what we do, we cannot manage behaviour as we would like. Starting with these ideas in mind means we can apply the practical strategies and techniques which follow with confidence and, crucially, with a strong rationale of how and why we believe they will work.

Behaviour as Communication

All behaviour which is apprehended by others communicates information, whether intentionally or not. Some of this communication is a direct result of what the person behaving does. Some of it is a result of the interpretations made by the person who apprehends it.

As an aside, I use the term apprehend deliberately because, while we come to know of other people's behaviour predominantly through sight (or a combination of sight and other senses), we can also learn of it without seeing the behaviour first-hand. We might see the results of someone's behaviour, hear someone else talking about a third person's behaviour, read about someone's behaviour and so on.

Much behaviour has the intention of communicating messages. For example, I might stand up to greet you when you enter a room in order to communicate respect and friendship. Or, I might cross my arms when someone is telling me something I don't want to hear, communicating displeasure and a closed-off attitude.

However, we are not always aware of the messages our behaviour communicates. This is particularly true of children and young adults who, as we have noted, are still learning about how to behave in the wider society and culture of which they are a part.

This can lead to problems.

A student may behave in a way which they believes communicates a certain message, whereas this message may be interpreted quite differently by the teacher who sees the behaviour. Alternatively, a student may engage in certain behaviour without even realising that this gives off a singularly unimpressive message.

We can contextualise this as follows:

A Year 9 student is bored in one of our lessons and wants the teacher to know this. They put their head on their desk as a result. The teacher sees this behaviour and interprets it as a direct challenge to their authority. This is because they see the student behaving in a way which is completely unacceptable in adult life.

Now, I am not suggesting that it is necessarily OK for the student to communicate their boredom (as adults, we know that boredom is a fact of life which has to be accepted at certain times). But, what we can see from the example is how, because they are learning about behaviour, students can sometimes fail to understand the actual content of the message their behaviour communicates.

In addition, we see here an illustration of the earlier point about the interpretation of behaviour. When we act, we are not in complete control of the communication those actions convey. This is because communication is always a two way street between audience and producer. You are reading this book and making your own interpretations of its content, just as I am writing with the intention of communicating my own thoughts and experiences as accurately as possible.

Two points follow from this.

First, we need to teach students what their behaviour communicates. Second, we need to be careful to moderate our own interpretations of student behaviour.

A different example will serve as further demonstration.

Let us imagine we are teaching a class of Year 3 children. In this group, one child takes a resource from another child without asking. They snatch it away, wanting to have it themselves. Here, we can see evidence of this child's lack of appreciation of an important norm underpinning group behaviour: we don't take things from others without asking. In dealing with the situation, we would naturally consider it important to explain to the child why what they have done is wrong.

In this process, we would be demonstrating (implicitly or explicitly depending on our use of language) that their behaviour communicated an inappropriate attitude, as well as a lack of consideration for other people's rights and feelings. Equally, we would know to moderate our own interpretation of the child's behaviour. This is because our experience would tell us that children of this age are wont to do things like this, are yet to develop an understanding of why it is not appropriate, do not act with the same volition as older children, and need to be regularly guided in terms of what is and what is not appropriate. We would also know that it is part of our job to correct their actions.

So, in the context of the classroom, the communication expressed by children's behaviour needs to be analysed and responded to in specific ways. This links again to our earlier ideas that behaviour is and can be learned and that part of our job is to teach it through the things we do in class.

Motives – Reason and Emotion

It is now worth thinking a little more deeply about why we act.

Earlier, we noted that we can divide the causes of behaviour into three categories: external, internal and a combination of the two.

Another way to think about the cause of behaviour is to talk in terms of motives.

Motives are the internal factors which can be said to drive our behaviour. When we say we are motivated to do something, we refer to the fact that something inside of us causes us to act. If we are demotivated, then the scope of our behaviour tends to reduce significantly.

Many philosophers, starting with Plato, have divided human motive into two broad categories: that of reason and that of emotion. The first category is concerned with our conscious, rational mind. That is, the part of ourselves through which we reason, analyse, pass judgement and, usually, seek to make decisions.

The second category is concerned with our passions. That is, the underlying sentiments which form part of who we are and over which we may or may not have much control.

Plato described reason and emotion as two horses pulling us in different directions. By this I think he meant to characterise the fact that these two parts of ourselves do not operate in the same way, and that, often, it might seem like following one way of thinking can cause us to deny or attempt to suppress the other. It follows that the best course of action might be the one which reconciles both aspects of ourselves – so that the two horses end up acting in pursuit of the same goal.

The Enlightenment philosopher David Hume suggested that reason is a slave of the passions. By this I take him to mean that any rational decision we choose to make is ultimately predicated on the things we desire, and that these flow from our emotions or sentiments.

We can take much from both positions to help us think critically about behaviour in the classroom.

Starting with Plato, it is fair to say that we all acknowledge the importance of teaching students how to prioritise their rational mind over their emotional one. This is not to the detriment of the latter, but as a means by which we can all live together successfully in local communities and wider society.

We know, roughly, that the prefrontal cortex is a part of the brain which develops during the period of early childhood to provide a moral, social buffer to the passions sparked by other elements of the brain. This explains why children at the age of around two can be surprisingly aggressive. They have, as yet, not developed the capacity to control their aggression – a necessary requisite for living successfully as part of a social group.

However, we also know that an individual who operates without reference to emotions is functionally abnormal. This tells us that some mid-point is preferable.

Students should have emotions and these will often be the motive for their actions, but these need to be exercised and fulfilled in the context of what is acceptable in wider culture and society. Restraint needs to be learned. As does rational decision-making. As does the consequence of letting emotions exert too much control over our behaviour.

Turning to Hume, we may reasonably accept that his argument is true. It seems a hard position to defend to say that reason can exist in the mouths of men and women without at least some connection to the sentiments which make us who we are. After all, without sentiments, what kind of a person would we be? Would we be a person at all? And, furthermore, is it not true to say that few people act deliberately against their own interests on all occasions?

These points briefly and inexpertly suggest the fact that Hume's argument holds for much of our experience. At root, the reasons we use to make decisions are exercised in relation to the underlying sentiments we wish to fulfil.

Connecting this to the classroom, we find ourselves thinking of students as being driven by underlying emotions, albeit with these generally manifesting themselves through rational action. But so too do we conceive of students as similar to ourselves, if at an earlier stage of development, given as how Hume's argument is universal in its application.

So where does this all leave us?

Well, I would suggest three points we can take away:

i) Our actions are governed by motives.

ii) These motives are emotional or rational in basis (arguably always the former, at root).

iii) Thinking about motives can help us to better understand why students act as they do.

Motives – Means, Ends and Goals

Leading on from this, we can say that motives are the basis for action and that, often, motives have as their aim their own fulfilment. For example, if I have the motive of acquiring good grades, I will achieve that end by acquiring good grades. And, if I have the motive of disrupting the lesson, I will achieve this by seeing the lesson disrupted.

Frequently then, motives are ends in themselves:

He was motivated by revenge and he achieved his revenge.

She was motivated by a desire to do good and this she did.

They were motivated to be successful and their grades gave them evidence they had achieved this.

In each of these cases, the people's behaviour is the means through which they achieve their goal; through which they fulfil their motive. Seen in this way, we can see why considering motive can be so important. It is the driving force of behaviour because it is through behaviour that motives can be achieved.

Two things follow. First, if we are for some reason prevented from achieving our goals, we may become frustrated. The degree of this frustration can vary tremendously and is dependent on a large number of factors. However, one thing we can take away is that students' poor behaviour can be a result of them trying to fulfil certain motives. If we act to deal with this, we may sometimes find ourselves facing students who then become frustrated.

Second, we all possess a mass of different motives, with these prioritised in different ways at different times. As a basic example, consider how the relative importance of different motives changes as you grow tired. Our body tells us that sleep is necessary and, commonly, this results in other motives being pushed onto the backburner, at least until we have regained our strength.

That we possess different motives has a couple of consequences. On the one hand, we as teachers can encourage students to focus on positive motives rather than negative ones. On the other hand, we can help students to be successful in achieving positive motives; helping them to act in a way which fulfils a goal we both share.

Once more, this takes us back to our by now familiar points that behaviour is and can be learned, that it is changeable and that, through our actions, we can teach students how to behave well.

It also suggests a few practical pointers (to which we will return later in the book) to underpin our behaviour management:

- Regularly communicating positive goals is a good way to habituate students into seeing these as worthy of their focus. This helps raise up the motive of achieving such goals, making it more likely that students will act accordingly.

- Many students, if not all, possess the various motives of wanting to do well, of wanting to succeed, of gaining some degree of status, and of being viewed as an individual, important and meaningful in their own right. These are all motives we can help students to fulfil. If they are able to fulfil them in our classroom, they will become positively disposed to our lessons – and their behaviour will likely be good as a result.

- We can show students the relationship between their behaviour (means) and what they want to achieve (ends, goals, fulfilment of motives). Put another way, we can show students the consequences of their actions and tie this to their own motives. This is a powerful tool through which to mould and develop the behaviour in which students engage.

Behaviour, Children and Young Adults

In the previous two sections, we highlighted some of the key similarities which lie beneath everybody's behaviour – young and old alike. This included the differing roles played by reason and emotion, as well as the characterisation of these different forces as motives, with emotion suggested as more powerful, or more likely to be found at the base of our decisions, than reason. We also noted the need to control emotion so that we can live together successfully, although this was accompanied by a clear sense that we learn this over time (thus, it is something we all share in general, but not something which manifests itself identically at all ages).

Yet, for all these similarities, it is vitally important to remember that behaviour does mean something slightly different in the context of children and young adults compared to what it means for the rest of us.

First and foremost this refers to the fact that the students we teach are in a developmental stage of their lives. They are learning. And, as we have noted, our teaching covers not just the content of the curriculum but the norms and values of society and culture as well.

While we want students to move towards a standard of behaviour which is indicative of the adult world, and indeed, to display such standards in the classroom as much as possible, it is also true to say that our motives should be tempered by a realisation that students will, at times, fall short – and that this is inevitable.

How could it otherwise be the case?

We can say with absolute certainty that boundaries will always be tested, that there will always be behaviour which is contrary to what we want, and that some expectations will end up being missed.

This is part of growing up. We've all been there and, to varying extents, exhibited behaviour as a child or young adult which we would not expect of ourselves as a grown-up. None of this is to excuse poor behaviour. Far from it. But it does serve as a reminder that the pursuit of excellent standards is a continuous process. Throughout our teaching, during every lesson we teach, we need to be aware that we are always faced with the task of managing behaviour.

Or, to put it another way, from the moment they enter the education system to the moment they leave, students are developing a knowledge and understanding of how to act, as well as what the consequences of their actions will be.

The point is further emphasised by the fact that, for many of us, looking back on our late teens and twenties we see that we were still learning – still developing – albeit in somewhat different contexts. And then there is the further argument that, while we come to gain a fairly sound general understanding of behaviour as we reach the end of our formative years, we continue to learn and to modify our behaviour throughout the entirety of our lives.

The second point to note is that, at different stages of development, various psychological and biological factors come into play as an influence on students' behaviour which we, as adults, have long past (and potentially forgotten about).

Hormones are the most obvious example. While many adults speak wistfully of the desire to be a teenager once again, such thoughts are often bathed in a warm nostalgia which carefully glosses over the tumultuous hormonal experiences which go hand-in-hand with this period of development.

Again, the point is not to provide an excuse for poor behaviour, but to offer further explanation of the forces shaping students' decision-making. Remembering to think about these forces and take them into account when managing behaviour can make the whole business much easier – as well as much simpler. In large part this is because we have some reasonable means to explain that which, at first glance, appears irrational to us.

But the characterisation of irrationality often prevents us from gaining an insight into the thought processes of the person whose actions we are judging. For, most people believe that the things they do are based on logical reasons. That is, choices which follow from prior premises. This is why many people deemed irrational are able to explain why they did things, and for this to have coherency within the set of boundaries they posit.

Here is the crux though – the last part of the last sentence: within the boundaries they posit. This identifies the fact that much irrational behaviour seems rational to the individual who carried it out because they are working with premises from which their subsequent decisions appear to follow logically.

Thus, a hormonal teenager may behave both irrationally and rationally, in that their behaviour appears irrational to us but rational to them. Knowing this makes it a lot easier for us to bridge the divide and to help students understand why, although they might feel what they have done is acceptable, it is in fact unacceptable when viewed from a different perspective.

As ever, knowledge is power and, in terms of behaviour management, having at least a working knowledge of child and cognitive development allows you to appreciate and unravel some, if not all, of the behaviour which might at first seems surprising.

Learning and Behaviour

In this final section we can draw together the various points raised so far and link these back to learning. This will provide us with a classroom-focussed summary which can act as the foundation for our practical strategies and techniques.

As teachers, our primary aim is to make learning happen. We want our students to know more and understand more than they did when they entered the classroom. We want to teach them. To open their minds, expand their horizons and help them to make great progress.

That is the key motive animating our actions.

Many students share this motive, but not all. Many students prioritise this motive over others, but not all. Many students want to learn and succeed but don't yet have the means to ensure their behaviour always supports them in this goal.

The most effective learning takes place in a classroom where behaviour is well-managed. This does not necessarily mean that the teacher has complete and total control. It does mean, however, that the teacher is continuously working to create and sustain an environment in which learning is everybody's focus.

Part of this involves planning and teaching great lessons. Part of it also means recognising the role we have to play in confidently and assertively teaching students what great behaviour looks like. This teaching will sometimes encompass the reinforcement of existing ways of acting, and it will sometimes involve changing how students act.

This is easier to achieve if we give some thought to the motives from which behaviour stems and the fact that, developmentally, students are experiencing a whole raft of psychological and biological changes which can influence their thinking and their actions. The corollary of this is that it is helpful to acknowledge the similarities between ourselves and our students, in terms of how we think and act, as well as the differences. And to distinguish the role the differences can play in causing, if not necessarily condoning, behaviour we might not expect from adults.

Ultimately, successful behaviour management rests on a belief that we can achieve the standard of student interaction and focus we desire. It might not be easy, but we must begin with a belief that it is possible. This rests on the twin premises that behaviour is learned and, as a result, can be changed; just as our wider teaching rests on the twin premises that all students can learn and, as a result, see their knowledge and understanding change. That we go about achieving these two goals – excellent behaviour and the development of knowledge and understanding – in slightly different ways is a given. That they are interconnected is also taken as beyond doubt.

So, with a firm foundation on which our thinking about behaviour can rest, we may turn to the practical tools with confidence and a clear sense of purpose.

That is what we will now do, following a brief summary provided for ease of reference:

- Behaviour refers to our external actions – it includes the things we do and say.

- Behaviour is caused. These causes can be internal, external or a combination of both.

- Behaviour communicates messages. Some of these are clear, some ambiguous. Some intended, some not. Some known by the individual whose behaviour we observe, some not.

- All messages are interpreted. Interpretations may differ from what was intended.

- Much behaviour stems from motives, with these being rooted in reason, emotion and sentiments.

- Children and young adults are learning. Their development includes learning about behaviour – every teacher is a teacher of more than just the curriculum

- The behaviour of children and young adults is malleable and open to change.

Chapter Two – Norms, Values, Roles and Status

The classroom is a social setting. It contains the integral elements of culture and society. Things we usually take for granted. Attending to these and using them as the basis for practical interventions is the first step towards developing excellent behaviour management.

This involves taking something of a sociological approach. Sociology aims to understand the nature of culture and society: those elements of which it is constituted and the relationship between these and the individual.

In the first three sections which follow, we will analyse this, providing some guiding principles before examining how we can apply these.

Society and Culture

These are two different things. Put broadly, society is the collection of families and individuals living together within a given area, usually a political entity defined as a nation state; and culture is the way of life of a group, including their norms, values, roles and attribution of status. The people living within a society may have a shared culture, or there may be a dominant culture, a series of overlapping cultures, or a series of distinct cultures which operate side by side.

We tend to take our own culture for granted. This is because we are so familiar with it. It is the reasoning which gives rise to the old maxim: 'Travel broadens the mind.' It does so in large part because it gives us access to cultures – ways of life – different from our own. In so doing it presents us with an insight at the same time as it suggests a comparison. That comparison is between what we are familiar with (our own culture) and what we have come to know (another culture).

Arguably, being able to turn and look from a distance at the culture of which we are a part, and being able to do so while juxtaposing what we see with another way of doing things, gives us the means by which to reassess how we live, for better or for worse. A changed context is akin to putting on a different set of spectacles. We see things differently as a result, sometimes to our surprise; sometimes to our chagrin.

The term culture can also be used to describe a smaller section of a way of life. So, for example, we might hear of a 'long-hours culture,' 'fan culture,' or 'a culture of neglect.'

When used in this way, the wider meaning of culture I have outlined above (there are other definitions available, though the debate surrounding these is of no use to us here) is pared down to mean a way of doing things in a certain setting or as part of a certain group. We might describe the usage as signifying a way of life within a broader way of life. I hesitate to use the word subculture here, because that refers to specific subsections of society who, in part, define themselves against the majority culture.

So let us continue with this idea that culture can be used to define both a general way of life and to denote the way things are done in a certain setting or group.

If the former usage cover the norms, values, roles and status which permeate the thoughts and actions of a large group, then the latter covers the norms, values, roles and status which are common to a smaller group or setting.

So it is that we can talk about the culture of a classroom. The culture of our classroom.

We said at the start of this section that the classroom is a social setting. That setting possesses a culture of its own. This may closely mirror the wider culture of the school, or it may be distinct. It may be closely tied to the wishes and intentions of the teacher, or it may not. But, being a culture of some sort, it contains a set of norms and values, as well as roles and means through which status is attributed or achieved.

Behaviour management is therefore centrally concerned with the creation and maintenance of the culture you want. A culture for learning. A culture composed of the norms, values, roles and status that helps to achieve this.

Norms and Values

Norms are unwritten rules. Values are the beliefs we think are important. Norms are usually based on values. For example, a norm in British culture is to queue up in an orderly fashion in shops, at bus stops and so forth. This derives from a few values, not least of which are the beliefs that politeness and fairness are important.

If people break norms, they may be considered deviant. The extent to which they are depends on the norm they have broken, the extent to which they have broken it and the concomitant judgement of their peers (or, sometimes, society). This indicates the fact that not all deviance is the same, and that not all norms are equally important. Thus, if I eat my boiled egg with a knife my friends may think me slightly odd, but if I take to shouting at the top of my voice while at work, I am likely to face a rather more significant response from those around me.

Deviance is often responded to through the exertion of social control. This can be formal (laws, police, prison) or informal (everything else). The latter includes things such as disapproving looks, shaming, isolation, telling off, avoidance and so forth. All those things which seek to reinforce and sustain the boundaries of what is deemed acceptable and appropriate in social life.

Norms can change, as can values.

In Britain, homosexuality used to be seen as deviant. Now it is not seen this way (in large part, though unfortunately homophobia does remain a part of our culture). Taking photos of yourself used to be fairly rare. Now selfies are ubiquitous. Shopping online was unheard of twenty years ago. Now it is an entrenched, ever-increasing norm.

In using these three examples I do not intend to draw a similarity between the first and the subsequent two. That would trivialise something of deep importance that has had a profound effect on many people's lives. Rather, my intention is to illustrate the extent to which behaviour in a society can change over varying periods, and the relative profundity and banality this can encompass.

When it comes to values, change can sometimes be a little harder to judge (because thoughts are unseen, meaning we rely on communication of these, often through changing behaviour, to be able to bear witness to changing values). We can note that in the three examples above, the first is undoubtedly a consequence of changing values, particularly in relation to the rights and freedom of the individual. The second is perhaps partial evidence of greater value being placed on individualism and identity, or on the importance of personal technology. And the third arguably reflects a value which has not changed a great deal in the post-war period: the desire for goods and services to make our lives easier and more enjoyable.

If norms and values can change, however, it means that any and all cultures are malleable. That they are is demonstrated by the time and tides of history. That the extent of their malleability differs can be seen simply by comparing two or more cultures in today's world with which you are familiar.

Of course, to say that a culture is malleable is not to say that it can be changed easily or completely, just to say that at least parts of it can be changed and that, on a wider scale, norms and values are not set in stone. They are social constructions.

This means that you can construct the norms and values of your classroom.

And these norms and values will define the culture you seek to create.

Deciding what you want, communicating this to students and then working to make it a reality is what behaviour management is all about.

And if you don't set, define and maintain the norms and values of your classroom, who will?

Roles and Status

We all have roles. Teacher, student, parent, friend, sibling, manager. Most of us have multiple roles.

In any culture, whether it be the larger culture of which we are a part or a more specific culture, such the culture of our classroom, different roles come loaded with different expectations. These expectations are usually in the form of norms we expect the role-holder to fulfil and values we think they ought to uphold. While there may be competing visions of what roles should entail, there is usually a great deal of overlap between these.

Two examples will help to illustrate the point – one writ large and one writ on a smaller scale.

In the United Kingdom, the society to which that name refers, the role of Prime Minister exists. Whoever takes on that role is expected to behave in certain ways. There are competing views as to what this ought to entail, but even the most disparate positions (that agree the role should continue to exist) have a great deal of common ground. Anybody who becomes Prime Minister knows they will have scope to make the job their own, but that this scope will be limited by expectations connected with the role. In the case of the Prime Minister these cover things like duties, ways of behaving in public, working for the national interest and so on.

All of us play the role of 'friend' for part of our lives. This role comes with expectations; norms and values which if broken bring into question whether we are indeed a friend or not. Asking one hundred people to define the role of 'friend' might produce a hundred different responses, with associated norms and values varying considerably. But we can be fairly confident that all the responses would retain a central core of similarity, given as how there is widespread agreement on the general nature of friendship in our society.

Now, let us draw this down to the classroom.

There, two roles stand out above all others: teacher and student.

The nature of these roles will differ depending on the age group you teach.

The norms and values associated with students in Year 3 will be different in many places from those associated with Year 13 students. However, there will once again be overlap. (On a side point, we might not call children in younger years students, preferring pupils or learners instead. Whatever the nomenclature, however, the point remains the same.)

In the previous section, we noted that, in your classroom, it is for you to establish the culture and that you can do this by defining, communicating and maintaining the norms and values you want.

Here, we can develop this point to say that this process ought also to encompass the definition of what you expect from yourself in the role of teacher and from the children you teach in the role of students (pupils/learners).

Doing this means developing a clear understanding of how the norms and values you set out translate into the specific roles played while teaching and learning happen.

This is important for a number of reasons.

First, clarity is key when it comes to behaviour management. Everybody needs to know where they stand, what is expected and why. If you can give clear guidance to yourself and to your students about what should be happening every time you work together, then behaviour management will become a much simpler task.

Second, students are at a disadvantage if they do not know what you expect from them in their role as students. They will not have the information necessary to tailor their efforts. They may be able to infer this, or they may pick it up over time, but why risk it? Life is much easier for you and for them if the criteria for successful, positive, learning-focussed behaviour are outlined and communicated from the off.

Finally, it is easier to cultivate norms and values if you can hang them on a role. For example: 'This is what I am looking for from a fantastic student. That's what I know you can be.' Here we see how we are providing something concrete children can grab onto. Instead of having to remember a long list of norms and values they can remember the role of student, connecting the varied and disparate elements to this single, memorable conceit. It provides a locus through which expectations can be communicated and remembered.

All of this leads us to our fourth and final element of culture: status.

Status is the recognition, rank and standing we possess. Status may be achieved or ascribed. In the first case, consider how you have achieved your status as a teacher. In the second case, consider how your gender and family name were ascribed to you at birth, or how children of members of the Royal Family have the status of royalty ascribed to them from birth.

Our status can and often does vary depending on the circumstances in which we find ourselves. I have one status at school, another at home. I have one status when I am with my friends, another within my family.

Some people strive for high status.

Everybody desires some level of status.

To be denied status is an unpleasant, possibly painful, experience. When it comes to children it often manifests itself in the form of neglect or abuse, with the neglecter or abuser depriving the child of the status to which they are entitled as a human being and which we, as a society and a culture, believe is inherent to all individuals, regardless of who they are (this frequently manifests itself in a belief in human rights).

Denial of status can also be less extreme, though still a negative experience. It can often be frustrating or humiliating to the individual in question. Many sporting groups (and some military ones) have been criticised for the way in which their so-called initiation ceremonies deliberately set out to temporarily demolish the status of the person being initiated.

We can also think of how people who bully others operate. They seek to undermine and deny the status of those whom they bully. It is through this process that they gain access to the power (status) which has often been denied to them in other areas of their life.

I use these three uncomfortable examples to highlight a couple of important points about status.

First, its denial or withholding can be used as a form of power. This gives credence to the argument earlier stated that we all desire some level of status. This acknowledgement of personhood – of our value as an individual – within the group of which we are a part would not be of importance if its denial or withholding had no effect. The fact that it does illustrates that it is something which matters, to all of us.

Second, if our desire for status is frustrated, we may seek it in other ways. And these may not be positive. This is often the case with people who bully others. It may also be evident in a student who is labelled as a failure and comes to regard themselves as such. If they believe the label which somebody has attached to them it follows that they will not believe they can achieve status through the traditional classroom route. As a result they may seek it through other means – by taking on the role of class clown, by disengaging or by being disruptive.

Third, there is a hugely positive point attached to the universal desire for status. As teachers, we are in a position to help all our students gain status. We can help all of them to learn, grow and achieve. To be successful and to fulfil the roles we set out for them.

All this leads us to the following:

- We should consider the opportunities we provide through which students can gain status in our classrooms;

- We should think about the way in which this status is connected to positive, learning-focussed behaviour;

- We should pay close attention to whether this status is achievable and accessible to all.

It is not about the teacher conferring status like a glorified potentate; it is about the teacher helping their students to gain the status which learning – in all its forms – gives rise to, as well that derived from being a positive, productive member of a group.

A final example to conclude this section. We are all familiar with the technique of improving the behaviour of a student by giving them responsibility. The responsibility does not have to be huge. It is the form of the gesture rather than its content which is indicative of status. The content plays a role, but the form (the attribution of responsibility with the concomitant implication that the student to whom it is attributed both deserves it and is capable of carrying it off successfully) is the key. The vignette shows us how something perhaps caused by frustrated attempts to gain status (poor behaviour) can be arrested by the achieving of status.

The point follows more widely.

It also indicates why students in purposeful classrooms often seem happier and more at ease than those in classrooms of the opposite type. In such classrooms, the path to achievement is clear; all students can travel along it with relative ease. Put another way, learning becomes everybody's business and everybody feels they can learn accordingly.

The Culture of your Classroom

To summarise the above thoughts we can say the following:

- The culture of your classroom is yours to define, communicate and maintain.

- If you don't do this, there will be a vacuum.

- The culture of your classroom includes norms, values and roles as well as the manner in which status can be achieved.

- Students may not share the norms and values you seek. But, as we noted in Chapter 1, behaviour can be learned and changed.

- Hanging your norms and values on clearly-defined roles makes it easier to habituate students into following them.

- You should also define your own role and communicate this to students.

- Status is not to be overlooked. You should plan ways to help all students achieve it in the context of learning and achievement.

We will now look at some practical examples of how to apply these general principles.

High Expectations

The number one way through which you can inculcate a positive, learning-focussed culture in your classroom is through high expectations.

Expectations are the predictions we make about the world. They are an attempt to know the future and, depending on what that future brings, may prove to be true or false. In the context of the classroom we find a crucial difference regarding expectations compared to life more generally.

When it comes to life in general, our expectations have a significant impact on how we behave and the ways in which we interact with other people, the experiences we have and the world we inhabit. However, our expectations tend not to have a significant impact on the world at large. Their scope of effect is limited.

In the classroom, things are a little different

The students we teach are constantly learning. Their minds are more malleable and plastic than our own. This reflects the fact that they are at an earlier stage of development than we are (though, I hasten to add, our own minds are still open to change, growth and alteration). Therefore, the expectations we convey to them will likely be taken on board as new information; they will be assimilated into their burgeoning knowledge and understanding of the world. They will have an impact.

The point is further reinforced by the fact that students, in general, will respond in kind to the leadership with which they are faced. This reflects the points we made earlier about behaviour being learned, being open to change and the role of habituation within this.

From here we can say:

- In the classroom, expectations have an impact.

- They represent information which students assimilate.

- The quality and content of this information will influence what students do and how they think.

If you have low expectations, students will take this on board and work with it.

If you have high expectations, the same will be true.

So go with the latter!

And know, in doing so, that you are giving your students information through everything you do; and that this communicates what you think they are capable of achieving.

Every part of your teaching, planning and assessment is an opportunity to model and communicate high expectations. Each occasion will work to reinforce the norms, values, roles and status you wish to prioritise in your classroom. So, for example, if you consistently expect students to apply maximum effort through the entirety of the lesson, then you will be communicating the fact that doing this is the norm in your classroom, that it is a part of the role of student, that status can be achieved by doing it, and that it rests on the values of independence and hard work.

Maintaining high expectations at all times allows you to be certain that you are always working to foster and sustain a classroom culture which reflects the kind of behaviour, attitude and application you want. If ever you are unsure as to whether what you are doing is sufficiently focussed on this, simply ask yourself if the expectations you are communicating are high enough. If you feel they are, rest assured that you are on the right track. If you feel they are not, identify where you can raise them and how you can communicate this.

Many of the strategies included in the following chapters will help you to convey and sustain high expectations. Knowing this is what they do and that this is what you are aiming for will increase their efficacy. You will be able to use them more effectively by virtue of understanding the meaning on which they rest.

Specifying Norms and Values in your Classroom

When seeking to develop excellent behaviour management, it is a good idea to sit down and work out what norms you want to see in your classroom and what values you feel are most important in the context of teaching and learning. Having done this, you should then seek to rank these, so as to provide yourself with a clear sense of what is most important and why. Some norms and values may be of equal importance to you, others may be relatively more or less important.

If you don't know what norms and values you want to promote, it will be harder for you to communicate clearly and consistently with your students. In addition, you may struggle to identify what it is you are trying to work towards. Having a good indication of the norms and values you want means having a sense of your ultimate goal: the behaviour you want to see day in and day out in your classroom.

It is also important to rank the norms and values, even if this is only roughly. Inevitably, there will be times when different norms and values come into conflict. For example, you might value both independence and respecting the authority of the teacher. On occasion, a situation might arise where these two values cannot both be fulfilled at the same time. Therefore, you will need to prioritise one and use this as the basis of your decision-making.

Deciding in advance what is most important to you means you have a critical lens through which to make decisions. While this cannot guarantee you will always make the right decision, it does increase the likelihood that you will. This is because your judgements will be founded on a prior analysis of what matters. As such, you can avoid the potentially damaging influence of spur-of-the-moment emotional reactions and also feel confident that the time you took to analyse matters in advance does not need to be repeated every time a difficult decision comes your way.

Here are three techniques you can use to help specify your desired norms and values:

- Visualise your ideal classroom. Think about what it looks like. Ask yourself what the students are doing, how they are working, what attitudes they display, the level of effort they put in, the characteristics of their behaviour, how they interact with you and each other, what the atmosphere looks like, the kind of work they produce, and the way in which they deal with setbacks. Doing this gives you your norms. It shows you what unwritten rules you would like your students to follow. Make a note of them, refine them if necessary, and then set about ranking them.

- Consider the different tasks and activities that will happen in your lessons. Think about starter, main and plenary activities, about group, pair and individual work. Think also about the times when you will be talking, about discussions and about the very start and end of your lessons. In each case, your aim is to bring to mind what you want, in an ideal world, in each of these situations. Doing so will give you a collection of norms. Some of these will be specific to certain lesson elements, others will be general. Make a note of them, refine them if necessary, and then set about ranking them. This method can be used as an alternative to that outlined above, or in conjunction.

- Sit in your classroom and look around the room. Imagine students coming in and out of there during the course of a year. Ask yourself the questions: What do I want to show students is important? What values do I want to teach them?

Doing this in context helps draw out the importance of values. It also makes it easier to connect essentially abstract concepts to the concrete reality of your classroom.

The process may take a bit longer than you expect. This is for two reasons. First, we take many of our beliefs for granted. This is because they are so much a part of our thinking that they can easily fade into the background. Second, articulating fundamental principles in which we believe and which we want to promote can be tricky. Capturing deep meaning within words is not always straightforward.

When you have your values, make a note of them and then rank them. Finally, ask yourself how you want to share these with students.

As an aside, one technique for establishing the values underpinning your thought is to look at the norms you want and to work backwards from there. This involves examining the reasoning upon which the norms rest. In so doing, you will be able to draw out the values which give ultimate meaning to the norms (warning: the results might cause you to question whether you still agree with the norms you originally set out!).

Specific Roles and Status in your Classroom

Having defined your norms and values using one or more of the methods explained above, you can then start constructing an outline of the role of student. You should decide what students need to do to be successful; what they will need to do to gain status in your lessons.

It is a good idea to think in general and specific terms and to connect together norms and values. So, for example, you might begin by identifying the general dispositions which will characterise a successful, learning-focussed student. Then, you might take each of these and distinguish a series of separate norms, each of which would give rise to behaviour indicative of the wider disposition. This is a process of categorisation and classification.

Possessing a clear sense of the role of student means you can share this information quickly and easily with your learners. This will help them to understand what you expect and to then live up to these expectations. It will also be a point of reference to which you can return through the course of the year.

In terms of status, defining and sharing what the role of student means gives learners a greater chance of being successful in your lessons and gaining the status they desire (with this status being a positive reflection of the teaching and learning you want to create).

Finally, we can turn to the role of teacher. To get a better sense of what you want yourself to be like in lessons, you should think about the norms and values you have defined for your students and then decide what you need to do to model these effectively.

Here we are working on the assumption that the teacher sets the standard for their students. This echoes what we said earlier about high expectations.

While the exact norms you attach to your own role will differ in places from the norms you expect students to follow, they will likely stem from the same values, overlap in places, and thus, as a result of these two points, model for students the standards you want them to meet.

The importance of defining the norms and values which attach to your own role can be illustrated by the imaginary case of a teacher who tells their students one thing and then does the other. Such a teacher sends out mixed messages. This inconsistency confuses students at the same time as it undermines any high expectations the teacher is trying to convey.

Excellent behaviour management sees consistency of purpose across the board. This gives students a clear sense of what is expected, backed up by teacher modelling and reinforced by the authority the teacher derives (the person who walks the walk has greater authority than the one who only talks the talk).

We can conclude the chapter by providing a summary of the points made:

- Culture is made up of norms, values, roles and status.

- Your classroom culture rests on what you define for each of these.

- Having defined what you want your classroom culture to be, you should communicate this clearly and consistently.

- Demonstrating high expectations at all times is an excellent way to do this. It should be the cornerstone of your behaviour management.

- Specifying the constituents of your classroom culture places you in a stronger position from which to communicate these. This, in turn, makes it easier for students to meet and exceed your expectations.

Chapter Three – Rules, Boundaries and Consistency

In this chapter we start to look at the mechanisms through which you can communicate your norms, values and roles to students, as well as the ways in which you can help them to gain positive status. This is the beginning of the tools of the trade you can employ to create the classroom culture you want; to make great learning happen by ensuring excellent behaviour.

Everything that follows is based on the assumption that you have followed the practical advice given in the previous chapter and defined what norms and values you want to cultivate in your classroom, alongside how these will manifest themselves in the roles students play and the concomitant relationship this all has to the achievement of status.

Why Rules Matter

We begin with rules. These matter because they regulate behaviour. Rules can be written or unwritten. In the latter case they are commonly referred to as norms. Arguably, rules govern every social situation in which we find ourselves.

Rules allow us to shape our behaviour so that it meets the expectations of others. They also allow us to predict the behaviour of those with whom we share a social space. This is because we work under the assumption that most people will also follow the rules, just as we do.

This assumption rests on a few points. First, the idea of reciprocity, meaning we anticipate that behaving in a certain way will result in others reciprocating. Second, the idea that most people will see the benefits which flow to all (including themselves) from following the rules. Third, that sanctions exist and will be enforced if rules are broken.

Being able to predict the future and successfully anticipate the behaviour of others makes life easier. We feel safe. We feel secure. We do not have to give our full attention to what is happening around us because we can be fairly confident that it is poses no risk to us. This allows us to focus on other things and to be productive.

In the classroom, rules bring about all these benefits. A classroom in which rules are known, shared, followed and understood sees students feeling safe and secure and able to focus their attention on their learning. The social aspect of the classroom experience becomes predictable and familiar, giving students the freedom to work harder and pile more of their effort into their learning.

Contrast this to a classroom in which rules are unclear, not enforced, unknown or not followed. Life becomes much harder for everybody. Students do not have a clear idea what is expected of them and are not able to predict the wider behaviour in the class with a high degree of accuracy. This decreases feelings of safety and security, pulls focus and effort away from learning, and means far more of the teacher's time is spent trying to create order.

While an effectively managed classroom does not need to be bound by a great iron cage of minor rules and myriad punishments for various infringements, it does need to contain a shared sense of what is acceptable and what is not, what will happen if the line of acceptability is crossed and why the rules – written, unwritten or both – benefit the group as whole.

Communicating Rules

To achieve this situation, you need to communicate the rules of your classroom. These will include the norms upon which you have decided, as well as perhaps some additional written rules connected to your values.

Here are five ways in which you can communicate rules effectively:

- At the start of the year, explain your rules to your students. As you do this, provide examples and explanation for each one. This will help students to understand and remember them, playing on the benefits of semantic interrogation (where we assign meaning in order to comprehend something and aid recall).

- Provide students with guidance on what a model student will think and act like. This sees you communicating your rules through the concrete example of the role you want learners in your class to assume. Continue this process by praising and drawing attention to examples of the role being successfully fulfilled.

- At the start of the year, lead students in a group discussion and development of a set of class rules. This is not for everybody but can be highly effective. This is because it binds students into the rule-creation process, quickly giving them a stake in the application and maintenance of the rules at the same time as it empowers them to feel part of proceedings.

- Display the rules of your classroom on your classroom walls and/or in student books. In the latter case, this can be done by sticking a sheet to the inside front cover. The advantage of this approach is that it gives you something tangible to refer to as and when necessary.

- During the course of your lessons, use every opportunity to communicate your expectations: through praise, modelling and the application of sanctions where appropriate. Recall that your expectations are an expression of the culture you want. Therefore, they implicitly communicate the rules you want students to follow.

It is likely you will use a combination of these. One on its own is unlikely to be enough. The fifth point indicates how communication of rules is an ongoing process. This reflects the continuous nature of social experience and the fact that, when working with children and young adults, it is to be expected that they will regularly test any boundaries you have set up.

The points above also further emphasise how important it is that you are clear in your own mind as to the rules of your classroom. If you are not, communicating these will be much more difficult.

Applying Rules Fairly

The application of rules is different to their communication. The latter concerns explanation, the former concerns use.

If your students follow all your rules from the get go, you will probably not have to apply them. Simply communicating them will have been sufficient. However, if rules are pushed against, transgressed or broken, then application will come into play.

When we talk of applying a rule we mean looking at a given situation and judging whether or not the rule has indeed been broken. If it has, we need to assess the extent of that breakage and then consider what the consequences should be for the individual or individuals in question.

If there is no consequence, the rule loses some or perhaps much of its force. The question becomes, in the minds of students, why bother following the rule if there are no consequences for not doing so?

If the consequences are too severe, the relationship you have with your students will likely deteriorate. You may also lose some authority (this usually derives in part from a feeling that you are a fair judge) and face challenges from your students. These challenges will likely be predicated on a sense of injustice, with students arguing, sometimes rightly, that the consequences meted out are disproportionate to the transgression.

Finally, if the consequences are inconsistent, you will face the biggest problems. This will completely undermine the purpose of the rules. Students will come to see their use as arbitrary; dependent on your whims and preferences (whether this is true or not) instead of reason, principle and precedent.

If all this sounds a somewhat highbrow description of how students think I would urge caution. From an early age we develop a sense of fairness and justice. This is acute in children and young people whose conceptual development is such that the world appears more black and white than it does to us as adults.

This leads to the conclusion that you should think carefully about how you apply your rules. Consistency is of utmost importance, followed by proportionality. The aim is to further support the manner in which rules work to regulate behaviour by regulating student expectations of what will happen if rules are broken. This means students will be able to predict with good accuracy what will happen if a transgression occurs.

Developing Rules with Students

In the section before last we touched briefly on the idea of developing rules with students. It is worth returning to this point here in a little more depth.

As noted, many teachers see this approach as an excellent way through which to promote a sense of agency and to bind students into the rules which are created. To that end, here are two approaches you might like to use too develop rules with your class:

- Divide the class into groups of three or four. Give each group a sheet of sugar paper. Display a silhouette of a person on the board and ask students to draw their own version in the centre of their sheets. Next, explain that groups have five minutes to annotate their images with the characteristics of an outstanding learner. You might like to give some specific examples to get students started and/or to display a set of categories on the board on which they can base their annotations.

When the time is up, pair groups together and get them to compare their 'outstanding students.' From here, you can move into a discussion in which the whole class agrees on their definition of an outstanding student, with this then forming the basis of the class rules. Everybody's subsequent aim is to meet or exceed the characteristics through what they do, what they say and how they act.

- Divide the class into pairs and display a selection of rules on the board which you think will help to create a positive learning environment. Invite pairs to discuss the rules. They should first decide whether they agree with them and what sort of behaviour they think they will give rise to. Next, ask students to come up with any rules of their own which aren't on the board but which they think are particularly important. Finally, challenge pairs to narrow down the rules to the five they think are most important for creating the right classroom culture. Indicate that students will need to justify their choices.

When sufficient time has passed, ask pairs to get into groups of four or six. In these new groups, students should share and debate their decisions before agreeing on five rules between them. Next, ask the groups to get together so that the class is divided into two roughly equal halves. Each half should repeat the process of sharing and discussing rules before deciding on an agreed set of five.

This will result in two large groups of students, each in possession of a set of five rules. Ask each group to appoint a spokesperson. These students take it in turns to read out the rules on which their group has agreed. You should then facilitate a debate between the two groups which leads to these two lists being merged into a final set of five rules. These become the golden rules of the classroom which all students must subsequently seek to meet.

Both these methods serve to engage students in the process of rule creation. In so doing, they help them to think about what good behaviour looks and feels like, as well as the foundations on which it rests. In addition, when you refer to the rules at a later date, you can do so while making reference to their origins and the role everybody played in this process. This is a powerful point through which to reinforce the social commitments students have to each other as members of the class.

Teaching through Rules

In Chapter 1 we looked at how the teacher's job encompasses both the teaching of the formal curriculum – knowledge and understanding connected to different subjects and topics – and the teaching of a hidden curriculum involving morality, how to behave and succeed in the wider world and other similar areas.

This reflects the fact that schools are both institutions designed to educate children and young people in the shared knowledge and understanding a culture has developed, as well as a place of transition between the world of the family and the world of society. They are an agent of socialisation serving a twin purpose.

As such, when we develop, communicate and apply rules, we are in fact teaching our students. This includes teaching them about the fundamental role of rules in culture and society, as well as what it means when rules are upheld, broken or ignored. If we manage behaviour well, we teach students a great deal more than the content of the curriculum.

We also teach them about the importance of self-control, self-discipline, teamwork and taking account of the expectations others have of us.

On the flipside, if we manage behaviour poorly, it will be much harder for us to help students develop this side of themselves – their character.

Thinking about the development, communication and application of rules as a means of teaching can help to temper our responses to students who challenge or break the rules.

Sometimes, emotion can get the better of us, causing us to respond harshly to behaviour we see as unacceptable. Granted, on occasions, it is important to demonstrate the severity of response certain behaviour can engender, though this is all the more powerful as a learning experience if it is rare.

A better approach is to think about how we can teach students through our example. This sees us remaining calm and assertive, carefully explaining to students why what they have done is wrong and what needs to happen to rectify the situation.

Dealing with rule-challenging and rule-breaking behaviour in this way means we are teaching students a wider truth about how culture and society believe conflict should be dealt with: through words, reason and discussion, rather than through anger or aggression. This harks back to the comments we made earlier regarding the developmental stages children and young adults are going through during their schooling, and the fact that they are still learning how to moderate and control their desires/passions/sentiments in order to become successful members of wider society.

Seeing rules as a prism through which teaching can happen will also help you to develop rapport with your students. This is because they will see your response to rule-challenging and rule-breaking as punitive *and* developmental, rather than simply the former. This reflects some of the deepest, oldest senses of what a teacher is: a guide who admonishes where necessary and supports wherever they can, always with the intention of doing their best for the students with whom they work.

Defining and Policing Boundaries

If we have rules, we have boundaries. These are the limits of acceptable behaviour. Not all rules have distinct boundaries. Some have fuzzy edges, with a zone of uncertainty after which the real boundary sits. Lying is a good example of this. We all agree that lying is wrong, but many people would also agree that white lies are often OK, particularly if they spare another person's feelings and do no harm.

Thus, the boundary of acceptable behaviour in relation to lying does not begin immediately at the point at which people start to lie. Instead, there is a zone of indeterminacy. Beyond this, there is a clear boundary we would all recognise covering things such as lying to cheat, lying to gain an unfair advantage, lying to cause harm to others and so forth.

To effectively police your boundaries, you need to define them. This means that you need to identify whether a zone of indeterminacy exists and, if it does, where it stops.

For example, one of your rules might be that all students should refrain from social conversation during the lesson. This might stem from the value that, in the classroom, learning must always take precedence. However, on reflection, you might decide that absolute enforcement of this boundary may be counterproductive. Therefore, you choose to have a boundary which means a little bit of social chat is acceptable, as long as it does not interfere with student work.

With this in mind, you would then be able to police the boundary while you are teaching, as well as communicate to your students how the rule works in practice.

Some rules will have very clear boundaries – no chewing gum in class, for example – while others will be less easy to define. It is this second class to which you should pay most attention, such that you know for certain where your boundaries lie (and can share this information with your students).

There are two more things to say about boundaries before we move on.

First, students want and need boundaries. These are the extents of the rules – written and unwritten – which matter in your classroom. The boundaries represent the extents of what is acceptable. If students don't know where they are, they will find it difficult to behave as you want them to and will struggle to predict behaviour – yours and that of their peers.

Second, as mentioned, children and young adults will test boundaries. In so doing, they are seeking to learn. Defining your boundaries in advance means you will be in a strong position when these tests come along. You will be able to tell students when they are getting close to the line and when they have crossed it. This is the information they seek. In addition, because you know your boundaries already, it will be much easier for you to maintain these in the face of any testing (compare this to a teacher who is uncertain over their boundaries and who, as a result, has them pushed back by students testing them...leading to poor behaviour and a difficult situation to resolve).

Defining and Using Sanctions

Effective rules and boundaries need sanctions. These are the consequences students will face if they transgress. Alongside sanctions sits praise, which we will put to one side and deal with in full in Chapter Five.

Sanctions are various in nature and include:

- Telling off a student

- Showing displeasure through body language

- Removing a privilege

- Giving a detention

- Showing disappointment

- Moving a student to sit somewhere else

- Giving a student different work to do

- Involving another member of staff such as tutor, head of year or senior leader

- Removing a student from the room

- Calling home to speak to parents

The severity of a sanction should reflect the severity of the incident. You should always leave yourself with somewhere to go. Starting off with severe sanctions will make life difficult as there will be nothing to move onto after this.

Defining your sanctions again involves doing a bit of work outside lessons, at the start of the year, to decide what consequences will follow from different types of behaviour. You should think carefully about this as it is imperative that you are able to follow through on your sanctions. If you can't, or if you don't, students will quickly realise they are hollow warnings. This will remove the risk associated with sanctions from any cost-benefit analysis they conduct regarding whether or not breaking the rules is worthwhile.

The result will be a higher incidence of rule-breaking alongside a sense of powerlessness on your own behalf as the sanctions you seek to employ do not have the effect intended.

Sanctions gain their effect from the following things:

- Being consistently applied

- Being carried out in full

- Being proportionate and tied to behaviour

- Being applied without fear or favour

- Being applied calmly, politely and assertively

The reasons for this are self-evident.

If a student refuses to change their behaviour in accordance with a sanction, you can escalate matters by applying a harsher sanction or by involving the school's wider behaviour system. In the latter case this could involve calling for help or putting the matter to one side and dealing with it after the lesson in conjunction with a relevant senior leader.

Whatever approach you opt for (and it may depend on the quality of the behaviour management system in your school) the important thing is to ensure that the sanction is applied, even if this takes time and effort on your part.

Never forget that sanctions play a significant part in maintaining rules and creating a sense of consistency. If you give up on attempting to apply a sanction for unacceptable rule-breaking behaviour, then you are communicating the message that the rule can be broken without any deleterious consequences.

Similarly, if you apply sanctions to one student but not to another, the inconsistency will once again diminish your authority, as well as the inherent authority students accord to the sanctions.

A difficult situation which can arise sees multiple students breaking a rule but you only catching one in the act. This means you can only apply a sanction to the student you catch, because you have no evidence regarding anybody else's behaviour.

The student in question may well argue that this is unfair – after all, they weren't the only one who was behaving wrongly, they just happened to be the only one caught.

This is hard to argue with. If true, the student is right in their assertion.

Therefore, avoid the argument. It will be hard, if not impossible, to win.

Instead, use the metaphor of a referee. Explain that you, like them, can only call what you see. You saw the student in question misbehaving and you are obliged to apply a sanction. You do not doubt that other misbehaviour may have occurred, but you do not have any evidence of this and therefore cannot act in relation to it.

This approach serves to defuse the situation by acknowledging the student's position while also reminding them that they were in the wrong and drawing attention to the fact that you are acting as fairly as possible given the evidence at your disposal, while not questioning the integrity of their argument (which may or may not be true, but which it will serve no benefit to challenge).

Sanctions: Good Practice

We can now look at three further examples of good practice when it comes to defining and using sanctions:

- If students know what consequences you have set out for rule-breaking behaviour and also know what rules are important in your classroom, then they have all the information necessary to behave appropriately. This is intensified if you go out of your way to continually communicate your high expectations to them.

From this we can deduce that accurate communication of information about sanctions is a key part of good practice. If students are not in possession of this information, they cannot reasonably be expected to behave as you would like them to. And, what is more, they will have a strong case from which to criticise you if and when you do apply sanctions (saying something along the lines of: 'Well, how was I supposed to know this would happen?').

- Non-verbal sanctions are an effective, non-disruptive means through which to redirect student behaviour, particularly that which represents a minor infringement of the classroom norms. In these cases, using body language and facial expressions serves to draw students' attention without making a big deal of the matter in question. In general, such gestures are hard to ignore. Many students will also appreciate the understated nature of your use of sanctions, rectifying their behaviour in accordance with your intimations and without need for further escalation.

- Regularly using minor sanctions such as body language, facial expressions, verbal reminders, gentle admonishments (for example: 'Remind me what great learning looks like in our classroom?') and redirections (for example: 'Stop doing that, thanks; back on task.') is an excellent way in which to avoid behaviour getting to a point where more serious sanctions need to be applied.

The principle here is one of proactivity. By focussing on the small things, and therefore the small sanctions, we stop the big things happening. To put it another way, by keeping the testing of rules and boundaries at the level of minor infringements, we make it less likely that major challenges will ever come about.

Sanctions: Bad Practice

Now to round out the picture by looking at a few examples of bad practice when it comes to sanctions:

- Applying harsh sanctions to a student in front of the whole class is a risky business, best avoided. Doing this places the student in question in a difficult position. They will naturally want to save face in front of their peers and so, regardless of whether or not the sanction is merited, are likely to escalate the situation by reacting in a negative manner.

While such situations are sometimes unavoidable, a number of alternatives are also available. First, we can ask the student to stop their behaviour and then go and apply the sanction later by talking to them one-to-one. Second, we can ask the student to step outside the room and to take a moment to think about their behaviour. Then, we can go and talk to them in a less charged setting, applying the sanction there. Finally, we can ask the student to stop their behaviour and then wait until the end of the lesson. At this point, we ask them to stay behind and talk to them quietly and calmly, again applying the sanction in a less charged environment.

- Starting out big. As mentioned, doing this leaves you with little room to manoeuvre. For example, a student might behave in a manner you regard as poor at which point you say something like: 'Do that again and I'll put you in detention for a week.'

Such a response is usually the result of an emotional reaction rather than rational thought. In the intensity of the classroom, this can often happen. Catching and stopping yourself is important though. In the above example, where else is there to go? And how likely is it that you will actually see the sanction through?

A good tip is to habituate yourself into a rule of three of approach. First, always ask the student to stop the undesired behaviour while indicating that it is detrimental to the learning happening in the class. Second, if the student does not stop, ask them again and this time indicate that a sanction will be forthcoming if they do not make a change. Third, if the student is still continuing in the behaviour, remind them that they have had two chances and then explain the sanction and apply it.

Note how I don't specify a sanction in this model. That's because I don't need to. You will have the time and space in which to decide on what would be appropriate during stages one and two. Then, if it gets to stage three, you are in a position to apply a reasonable, proportionate sanction you know you will be able to follow through on.

- Holding on to sanctions. The point of a sanction is that it is a consequence for rule-breaking behaviour. Holding on to it means punishing a student twice for the same act. First with the sanction. Second with the mindset you have about that student in which you continue to think of them in the context of the sanction.

This way of working leads to labelling. That is, the process whereby we stop seeing students as individuals and instead attach labels to them which we then use to characterise their entire behaviour. For example, you might hear a teacher in the staffroom describe a student as 'a regular little troublemaker.' This is bad. While the student may have been in trouble on a number of occasions, what chance have they got of changing their behaviour if teachers are viewing them through this prism?

When a sanction has been applied, it is time to move on. If the student in question breaks the rules again – particularly if they break the same rule – then we should return to the original sanction and ask whether it had the impact we anticipated. But, outside of that, we can't expect students to improve their behaviour unless we give them the space in which to do so.

Short-Term Pain for Long-Term Gain: Creating Habits Through Consistency

Everything outlined above, concerning rules, boundaries and sanctions, can be summed up in the context of our preceding chapter, where we examined the importance of establishing a classroom culture – the culture you want – through the identification of its constituent norms, values, roles and ways of achieving status:

Creating positive habits is key.

Rules help to do this by regulating behaviour. Boundaries help do it by defining the limits of what is acceptable and by giving meaning to rules in the classroom context. Sanctions help do it by providing consequences for breaking rules and pushing boundaries. Consistency of application underpins all this, creating a sense of certainty about what is expected and what is likely to happen if these expectations are not met (as well as what will happen if they are).

In the short-term, especially when you are first starting out with a class, this can result in some uncomfortable moments. You may also have to teach some lessons in a manner which runs counter to your preferred style.

This is because the emphasis in the short-term is on establishing a set of habits (indicative of the culture you want) and these may be new to students. If they are, this unfamiliarity can give rise to more challenges and transgressions than you might anticipate.

But remember that the whole experience is a learning process for students. And the information you communicate to them through everything you say and do will inform them as to the extent of the habits you wish to develop, the reasons why, and what you will do if this is achieved, if it is partially achieved or if it takes some time to achieve.

Communicating consistency means setting students up for long-term success, even if, in the short-term, some pupils rile against the rules, boundaries and sanctions you put in place. As they come to learn that you are consistent, however, they will be able to predict what is expected of them in your lessons and will come to know that working against this will not be accepted.

And all of this will be complemented by your simultaneous communication about learning, about the potential to make progress all students possess, and about the benefits to the group that great, learning-focussed behaviour brings.

In summary then:

- Rules need to be defined and communicated.

- Your rules should reflect the culture you want to create and should be applied fairly.

- Boundaries should be defined and communicated.

- Your boundaries should be tied to your rules and carefully policed.

- Sanctions should be defined and communicated.

- Your sanctions should be applied fairly and carefully and should always be followed through.

- Consistency in all the above is the key to training your students in good habits.

Chapter Four – Planning for Learning

In this chapter we turn our attention to the ways in which our planning can help us to expertly manage behaviour. We will look at a series of different strategies and techniques you can employ to ensure your planning stimulates and encourages positive, learning-focussed behaviour, helping you to develop the classroom culture you want.

Before we move onto this, we can briefly note that effective lesson planning is a fundamental feature of excellent behaviour management. This is because the behaviour students exhibit in your classroom is always within the context of a lesson you have planned. Therefore, effective lesson planning is more likely to encourage good behaviour.

For example, we might imagine a poorly-planned lesson in which the teacher has not given sufficient thought to what students will be doing and the level of challenge they will be asked to meet. On top of this, the teacher is not entirely sure themselves of how the lesson structure will play out in practice.

Two points follow. First, the better planned your lesson is, the more time you have free to attend to what is happening while you teach. Your mind is not caught between trying to work out how the lesson is going to move forward and what there is in front of you. Instead, you can focus on the latter, allowing you to do all the things necessary to ensure behaviour remains at a high level.

Second, having a clear understanding of what you expect students to do during a lesson, the learning this will involve and the level of challenge underpinning it means you know in advance the route the lesson ought to take. Therefore, you also know how to identify, in terms of behaviour, anything which deviates or takes away from this proposed journey.

Keeping behaviour in mind while planning your lessons will help you to realise these benefits. Forgetting about behaviour means decreasing the likelihood of realising them – you might achieve them or you might not, but you will not be working actively to make this a reality.

With these thoughts in mind, let us look at the specific, practical tools you can employ while you are planning your lessons.

Lesson Structure

The first thing to consider is lesson structure. When first sketching out your lesson, you should think about how the structure will influence the level of pace and challenge your students will experience. If the structure dulls either of these two areas, you can look to change this.

For example, you might sketch out a Year 7 lesson in which students need to do a lot of listening to the teacher in the first thirty minutes, before going on to apply the knowledge they gain from this. On reflection, this structure may well give rise to disengagement or demotivation. Thirty minutes is a long time for Year 7 students to sit and listen.

Picking up on this point early means you can rectify matters. Making changes before you get into the meat of your planning makes life much easier. In this case, you might decide to break up that first thirty minutes into two fifteen minutes sections with a paired discussion activity in between. This will play to students' strengths, giving them time to regain psychological energy they can then apply during the second section of teacher-led explanation.

Thinking about lesson structure means thinking about how the framework of your lesson can support or work against your behaviour objectives. As noted through the example, this rests in part on an analysis of the psychological impact of the lesson structure; the kind of feelings and responses it is likely to provoke in students.

The point is not to plan lessons that are endlessly responsive to the whims of students – that would be ridiculous. Rather, it is to consider the relationship between your lesson structure and the experience students will have – and to which they will respond and react.

Seating Plans

These are an essential part of effectively managing behaviour. The classroom is a social space. This gives rise to social interaction. Students interact differently with different peers. As such, you need to plan the seating in your classroom so it maximises students' focus on learning. This means thinking carefully about who will sit where and why, and what you will do if the seating plan you develop proves unsuccessful.

Things to avoid include:

- Groups of friends sitting together

- Students who need more teacher support sitting in inaccessible places

- Students prone to talking or behaving poorly grouped together

- Students prone to talking or behaving poorly sat near the back (or away from the teacher)

Things to think about include:

- Student eye-lines: who can see who and are they likely to interact poorly with them?

- Teacher eye-lines: Who can you easily see? Can you see everybody in the class?

- Table layout: Do you want rows, a horseshoe, pods or something else? How will your layout help or hinder behaviour management?

- Access: Can you easily access the students who are most likely to need your help?

Things to aim for include:

- Having a clear rationale behind the placement of all students

- Being prepared to make changes if the seating plan does not work out as expected

- Grouping students who experience, intuition or deduction tells you will work well together

- Seating students who will need support (including those who may need regular support with their behaviour) near the front and on the end of rows, so you can easily access them

- Minimising the opportunity for students to distract one another (for example, by avoiding eye-lines which may lead to off-topic conversation or disruption)

In conclusion, your seating plan is a powerful tool for managing the social dynamic within your classroom. It is an excellent way through which to set the tone of your lessons and through which to promote the learning-focussed culture you want.

Starter Activities

Different types of starter activities serve different ends when it comes to managing behaviour. Thinking about this when planning your lessons will help you to plan for excellent behaviour. Here are some examples:

- **Settlers**. These activities settle students, calming them and getting them to quickly focus on their learning. They tend to do this by setting an accessible, individual task which draws students' attention. For example, we might ask students to write a paragraph explaining their views on a topic, or to make a list of everything they remember from the previous lesson. Encouraging an individual focus means discouraging off-task behaviour and drawing students into the culture you want.

- **Exciters**. These activities immediately engage students and make them feel excited about being in the lesson. They are particularly good if you want to motivate a class and create a sense of positive momentum. This makes them useful if students are lethargic or apathetic. Examples include posing an unusual problem or question and giving a two-minute time limit in which students must develop a response with a partner; competitive or team-based games; and using an arresting image as a stimulus for paired discussion.

- **Routinized Activities**. Another approach involves routinizing your starter activities. This sees you developing a set routine which you embed in all your starter activities and which serves to bind students into the lesson through familiarity and recourse to past behaviour. For example, you might develop a routine by which students come in, copy down the lesson title, learning objective and key question, remind themselves of their current target and then attempt the starter activity. The obvious benefit of this approach is that it habituates students into a way of acting which is learning-focussed, giving you a chance to control the direction and atmosphere of the lesson from the outset.

- **Repeated Activities**. We can also bring the benefits of habituation to bear in terms of the activities we use. Identifying a suite of starters which help you to achieve the learning you want means you can then train students in how to respond to these starters. Over time, students will come to recognise the activity types and will be predisposed to interact with them based on their prior experience. This can help get your lessons off to a cleaner, quicker start.

The aim, then, is to give thought to the starter activities you plan, considering how these will influence your students, as well as the kind of lesson starts they will engender. More options exist than space permits me to outline, however those explained above will get you off to a good start(!).

Facilitating Success

Success is motivational. It gives us a sense of achievement and helps to promote a positive mindset; one which works through inductive logic to suggest: 'well we did that, so presumably we can do more too.'

For these reasons, ensuring all students can experience success in your starter activities is an excellent technique through which to promote engagement and a good start to your lessons. It binds learners into the learning, giving them a positive, motivational experience from the word go.

Of course, we do not want to make our starter activities so simple as to be completely unchallenging. Finding a balance is key.

An easy way to do this is to plan a two part starter activity. Part one should be based on the first two levels of Bloom's Taxonomy of Educational Objectives – knowledge and comprehension. Part two should be more challenging and therefore based on an extended degree of comprehension or on one of the higher levels (application, analysis, synthesis or evaluation). Here is an example from a Year 11 Psychology lesson introducing students to the topic of learning:

Starter Activity: Make a list of every word which comes to mind when you hear the term 'learning.' Try to include some scientific and psychological words on your list.

Challenge Question: Is learning possible without memory? Why?

Here, the main starter activity is predicated on knowledge and comprehension. We are asking students to recall things they already know and to do so by thinking through the lens of 'learning.' This is accessible for all, based on prior experience and allows everyone in the class to be successful and, therefore, to feel that they are a part of the lesson.

The challenge question is more demanding. Perhaps half the class will get onto it, perhaps all of them. Either way, students will have their thinking stretched as well as having the opportunity to experience immediate success. Thus, we achieve our twin aims of creating motivation and positive sentiment at the same time as we challenge students to think in depth about the topic.

This model can be applied to nearly any topic and age group.

Transitions

These are the moments when the lesson moves from one thing to another – when you make a transition. For example, we might make a transition from our starter activity to teacher explanation of the main activity followed by another transition to students engaging in the main activity.

Transitions are an inevitable part of any lesson. However, they do tend to disrupt the flow of the learning and, of course, offer an opportunity in which students might start to go off-topic.

As such, it is worth thinking about transitions during the planning process. First, you should look to minimise transitions. If you create a lesson containing a large number of these then you are making your life more difficult. At each transition you will have to manage the disruption of the lesson flow and exert energy keeping students focussed.

Fewer transitions means fewer breaks in learning. It also means less of your time devoted to managing these breaks.

Second, you should think about how you will glide over transitions, minimising any negative impact they might have. This means identifying ways in which you can hide or cover up transitions. They will still be there, underneath the surface, but students will not be aware of them.

For example, an unhidden transition might involve the teacher ending an activity and then spending thirty seconds changing their PowerPoint slide over and handing out a set of resources. In this situation, students see the transition and are likely to react or respond accordingly.

To hide such a transition, we could freeze the board five minutes earlier, have the next PowerPoint slide up and ready, and place the resources face down on students' desks before the first activity ends. This allows us to move the lesson on with barely a sense that we are transitioning from one section to another.

These are simple techniques yet extremely effective.

Attend to them during your planning and then, while you are teaching, remain five to ten minutes ahead of your students at all times, so that you can manage the transitions as efficiently as possible.

Thinking from the Students' Perspective

Having planned a lesson, it is always worthwhile spending a couple of minutes thinking it through from your students' perspective. This involves thinking about what students will be doing at each point of the lesson.

Doing this allows you to spot any of the following:

- Lesson segments when expectations are unclear

- Points at which students have nothing to do

- Sections during which some students are occupied but others are not

- Activities which may work for certain students but not for others

- Periods when the lesson pace is not as you want it

Having spotted such situations, you can deal with them by amending your lesson plan. This makes you better prepared for managing behaviour. It stands in contrast to the opposite approach, whereby we wait until we are teaching the lesson to see what students do and how they respond. While we cannot predict exactly how students will engage with the lesson, we can make reasonably accurate predictions and use these to adjust and modify our planning.

An additional point is to think through your lesson from the perspective of different groups of students. This might involve imagining yourself into the position of less-able, middle ability and more-able students, or students for whom English is an additional language or who have particular behavioural needs. In each case, you will gain an insight into the extent to which your lesson plan meets the needs of the students in question and gives them a good chance of behaving positively.

Organisation of Materials

If we are well organised we are more likely to be in control of our teaching. This is because our full attention can be focussed on what is in front of us – our students – and what we are trying to do – create great learning.

Lesson planning is itself an act of organisation. By developing a plan we are seeking to organise the time we have with students, segmenting this into a series of lesson sections which, in conjunction, serve to maximise progress.

An additional aspect is the organisation of materials. This refers to the slides you use for your lesson, any resources you need and, if appropriate, student books. Again, this is a basic point. However, if overlooked, lack of organisation in any of these areas puts you at a significant disadvantage. First, you will have to devote some of your time and energies during the lesson to dealing with the issue. Second, you will convey a message to students which may undermine other things you do.

For these reasons it is always preferable to print and photocopy resources the day before (wherever possible), to keep track of student books and to develop a routine for handing these out. In terms of the last point, you can do this yourself or train your class to do it, either as a group or via appointed book monitors.

To give an example of the benefits effective organisation can bring, consider the messages students receive when they enter a classroom in which the starter activity is already displayed on the board, books are on desks, waiting to be used, and resources and ready to go, stored in separate, easily accessed piles at the front of the classroom.

This returns us to our earlier thoughts on classroom culture, high expectations and the model that you provide for your students.

Activities Which Minimise Interactions

If we have a class where behaviour management is difficult and disruption a frequent occurrence, it is an excellent idea to adapt our planning so as to stop problems developing well in advance.

Asking students to work together – in groups or pairs – means ceding a degree of control over what is happening in the classroom. Often, this is an excellent thing to do; it is a great approach to learning which regularly yields fantastic results.

However, if you are struggling to get the kind of behaviour you want, then it usually stops being the best option to choose. This is because it undermines your wider attempts to gain control of the atmosphere in the room. Instead of helping you to do this, it gives students the freedom to continue in the negative behaviour patterns they have developed.

A better alternative in the short-term is to think about activities which minimise rather than promote interactions. While this might be antagonistic to your wider beliefs about teaching, the fact remains that group work and other such activities are only effective if students can be relied upon to behave in a positive, learning-focussed manner while they take part in them.

Our priority is to first get the classroom culture we want. We can then use this to facilitate a varied and exciting approach to teaching and learning.

Activities which minimise interactions include:

- Individual writing

- Answering a series of questions independently

- Reading (either standalone or with a set of related questions)

- Teacher-led discussion (in which the teacher speaks and then chooses one student at a time to add to the discussion)

- Teacher talk

- Making notes

- Creating individual products such as mind-maps, leaflets or guides

- Using a textbook

- Watching and making notes on a video (perhaps supplemented by a listening frame)

In all these cases, the activity serves to direct students away from interaction and towards the learning. This allows the teacher to exert control, to convey the message that learning is our focus above all else, and to reinforce the norms of interaction they want, in opposition to the norms under which students were previously operating.

Planning these types of activities will help you to regain control over a class whose behaviour is other than how you want it. Over time, you can slowly reintroduce other types of activities and judge the extent to which students can deal positively with these.

An additional benefit is that if you have a selection of activities which minimise interactions stored away you can call on these mid-lesson, if the need ever arises. So, for example, if a group work activity goes pear-shaped, you can swiftly amend your lesson plan and ask students to write up their thoughts individually. This will allow you to temper the atmosphere which has developed and to redirect students back to focussing on learning.

Training Students in Systems

We have touched briefly on the idea of training students. In this section and the next two, we will examine it in more detail. Throughout, the intention is that we set out with a plan to train students and then include the things in which we have trained them as part of our lessons.

Training students in systems means identifying the procedures you think will prove useful in your lessons before training learners in how to complete these. Examples include:

- How to start the lesson

- Giving out books and resources

- How to end the lesson

- How to give feedback

- How to do peer- and self-assessment

- How to answer questions

- What to do if you don't know what to do

- How to be independent (for example, by trying to work out an answer yourself, referring to a book and then asking a peer before coming to the teacher for help)

In each case, training involves showing students how you want the thing in question done and then giving them time to practice doing it. Three points follow. First, you will be able to call on the system again and again in future lessons. This will help regulate behaviour and will contribute to the culture you want. Second, students will be able to experience success through the correct application of the system; they will also develop a sense of familiarity with it which can be comforting. Third, the system will save time in the long-run, making your lessons more efficient as a result.

Some teachers like to train their students in a raft of systems in the first few lessons of the school year, challenging them to keep practising the application of these until they can follow them quickly and effectively with barely a second thought. This approach does not suit everybody but can be an excellent way to build rapport and communicate your expectations.

Training Students in Activities

This involves selecting a small collection of activities you then return to on a regular basis as part of your lesson planning. For each of these activities you train students in how to successfully complete the task, giving them opportunities to practise early on in the term.

Doing this allows students to learn how to successfully complete activities. As a result, when they meet the activities on subsequent occasions, they can give their full attention to the content of the tasks. This is because they do not have to spend time decoding your instructions or working out what it is they are supposed to be doing.

The benefits are clear to see. More learning will take place because students know what is expected of them, less disruption will arise due to uncertainty about what the learning entails, and students will get ever more efficient at the activities in question, allowing you to increase the level of challenge.

You can train students in all activity types – starters, main activities and plenaries. A good idea is to begin with a small set, as previously stated, and then, as students become familiar with these, to introduce one more at a time, allowing you to build up a wider selection of activities in which students are trained. This allows you to realise the benefits of familiarity and variety.

Training Students in Rules

Our final nod towards training concerns training students in rules. Here, we are thinking about how we can help students to learn off-by-heart what is expected of them at different points in our lessons.

To begin, break your lesson down into a series of separate parts. For example:

- The lesson start

- Main activities

- The lesson end

- Paired work

- Group work

- Individual work

- Discussion

For each of these sections, identify what rules you expect students to follow. If you have been through the processes outlined in earlier chapters concerning the identification and specification of your classroom culture this will take only a few moments.

Next, plan to give students a chance to learn these rules in the first few weeks of the year. This will involve explaining to students the different parts of the lesson you have delineated, as well as the rules you have assigned to each section.

For example, you might display the rules on the board prior to each lesson part and then remind students of these while they are working. Then, you may follow up with a brief review in which you and your students discuss the extent to which the rules were followed.

Another option is to create a handout containing information on the rules relevant to each lesson part, to print this off and give it to students, and to then refer to this regularly over the first few weeks of term. Doing this will help train students in the various rules you want them to follow.

In both examples, the aim is the same. Training students in what rules are relevant at different points of the lesson and in what meeting these involves makes it quicker and easier for them to live up to your expectations over the remainder of the year.

Identifying Issues of Access

Behaviour is caused by motives; thoughts, feelings, sentiments and reasoning lead us to do things and to say things. One of the most common causes of poor behaviour in lessons is the frustration students feel at not being able to access the learning.

This frustration can manifest itself in different ways. All stem from the student feeling they cannot achieve what they are being asked to do. This makes it hard for them to gain status in the context of the lesson, is demotivating, and may lead them to ask the questions: 'Why am I here?' and 'Why should I bother with this?'

You can work to prevent this problem arising while planning your lessons. Having created a lesson, look through the different things you are asking your class to do and think about these in relation to individual students. For each task, question or activity, ask yourself whether this might throw up an issue of access for certain students.

If it does, deal with it.

For example, you might identify that half-way through your lesson the level of challenge increases quite quickly. While this is for good reasons, you may also come to realise that it could act as a block for the less-able students you teach. Their ability to access the learning in the second half of the lesson will be less than that of their peers.

Having spotted this, you can plan to work with those students in a small group once you have set up the second half of the lesson and set the rest of the class on their way. Alternatively, you might decide to include a simpler sub-task which will scaffold the increase in challenge, with less-able students able to use this as a stepping-stone to help them access the more demanding content.

Thinking about student access to learning during the planning process will help you to iron out any problem points. This diminishes the possibility that poor behaviour will be stimulated by student frustration. It will also help you to maximise progress across the board.

Lock-Down Lessons

Sometimes, things do not go as we hope or expect. We have all had the experience of a class for whom behaviour is a major issue. In these situations, the balance between stimulating teaching and learning and ensuring we have some degree of control tips firmly in favour of the latter.

Our primary objective becomes stopping the negative behaviour which has developed. If we don't do this, little else of merit will ever be possible.

The first step in such situations is to break the cycle of learned behaviour. That is, to stop students associating the lesson with the norms and values they are operating under.

But this isn't easy. It requires time and persistence as we try to break down old habits and inculcate new ones.

To begin the process, lock-down lessons are particularly useful. They are a fall-back option we can keep in our lesson-planning locker, pulling it out on the rare occasions when behaviour is sufficiently poor that we deem radical change to be necessary.

A lock-down lesson is a lesson which has the express aim of minimising interactions, maximising teacher control and reasserting the primacy of learning over everything else. They need to be highly focussed and heavily directed. Here are some examples:

- Students work on a series of independent writing tasks for the whole lesson. Discussion is prohibited and the focus is strictly on the work students have in front of them.

- The teacher provides three subtitles and gives a lecture around each of these. Students listen and make notes. At the end of the lecture, students write up their notes individually and then answer a series of relevant questions.

- Students are given a set number of textbook pages to read and make notes on. This is followed by a series of questions to be answered independently, connected to the information in the textbook.

As you can see, in these three examples learning is still important but it comes second after behaviour. The aim of lock-down lessons is to subjugate all else to the maintenance of focus and the neutralisation of poor behaviour. For this reason, they are an excellent tool to be able to call on in times of need. Equally, if you follow and implement the advice in this book, you should rarely have need to call on them. Knowing they are there is always good, however.

To this end, you might like to sketch out two or three suitable 'lock-down lessons' relevant to the subject and/or age-group you teach. Planning these in advance means you will always have them to hand, should the need ever arise.

With that we conclude our examination of some of the ways in which we can plan for positive behaviour and great learning.

In summary:

- The lessons you plan have a major impact on student behaviour.

- Bearing this in mind allows you to plan more effectively.

- Ensuring students are able to experience success and that they have their thinking suitably challenge is always helpful.

- Understanding how students are likely to experience your lessons gives you a chance to make important changes in advance of teaching them.

- Thoughtful preparation and good organisation go a long way to helping you manage behaviour effectively.

A final point to note is that the information you elicit when you teach your lessons (how students respond, how they engage with the learning, how they deal with certain activities and so forth) is information you can use to inform any subsequent planning. This allows you to improve the quality of what you do, resulting in lesson plans which are increasingly effective in terms of how they help you to manage behaviour.

Chapter Five – Using Praise

Earlier we considered the importance of negative sanctions. These are the consequences which follow when rules are broken or norms transgressed. However, another set of sanctions exist, positive ones. This might seem strange at first. We tend to associate the word 'sanction' with the application of punitive measures.

Thinking about sanctions as potentially negative and positive helps us to remember the wide range of consequences we can make students aware of in relation to their behaviour. On the one hand we have negative consequences, on the other we have positive ones.

Included in the latter are such things as rewards and prizes. The most important element, though, is praise. This is reflected by the fact we have an entire chapter devoted to it. In this, we will first briefly examine the nature and power of praise before looking at the practical measures through which you can use it effectively.

The Power of Praise

Praise is powerful. It has an effect on people. It makes them feel good, can validate their actions and indicates the high esteem the deliverer of praise has for them and what they have done. Praise makes people feel important and recognised; it lets them know that their efforts have not gone unnoticed. Through this, praise can positively reinforce behaviour. We associate what we have said or done with the positive feelings receiving praise brings about, and so we repeat our actions.

Praise assigns status. When we praise somebody's actions, we are suggesting that what they have done should be taken as a positive thing. Such public affirmation is a signal of status being acknowledged. Consider, as an alternative, an individual who feels their efforts are always ignored and that they never receive the praise they believe they are due. This person would feel as if their status was being denied or sidelined.

It is no surprise that in many surveys of people at work, one of the top factors suggested as a way to improve motivation and morale is not additional money, but praise from a manager. Acknowledgement of our efforts has a major effect on how we see ourselves and how we believe other people see us.

To further illustrate the point, think back to a time you received a piece of praise that has stuck with you. How did it make you feel? Then, think of a time you observed another teacher giving a powerful piece of praise. How did this affect the student to whom it was directed?

There is an old saying that excellent motivators can make people feel ten feet tall. They do this through praise; by drawing the individual's attention to all the things which are good about them and which they can do well. Doing this fills the person with confidence, giving them a sense of their own worth and of the intrinsic value they possess. The validation which praise provides cannot be underestimated.

On top of this, we tend to feel positively disposed to those who praise us; flatterers attempt to make use of this psychological feature as a matter of course. If we feel positively towards someone, we are more likely to work hard for them, to follow their instructions and advice, and to believe that they have our best interests at heart.

In terms of behaviour management, praise allows you to reinforce the behaviour you want to see, helps you to build rapport with your students, provides an excellent model, generates a positive atmosphere in your classroom, and encourage students to appreciate that you and they are a team working towards a common goal.

Genuine, Specific Praise

When delivering praise, you should ensure it is genuine and specific. Students will quickly spot praise which is false. This will lead them to distrust subsequent praise you deliver, whether it is genuine or not.

To deliver genuine praise, you need to look at what students are doing and think about how one or more elements of this are good. And you need to do this regularly. Irregular praise may be viewed as suspect. It provokes the question: why now? This implies that the praise is being given for an ulterior motive, not as a result of habit.

Giving praise which is specific helps to increase the sense that it is genuine. This is why praise which is general or banal is often dismissed as so many empty platitudes. The argument is that any one of us could say those things as they do not require any effort. The content of the message has been lost on the back of overuse and repetition.

To demonstrate, compare these two pieces of praise:

A) Wonderful work today, Yolande, you are doing great.

B) Wonderful work today, Yolande, you kept going even when things were challenging. That's what we want to see.

There is nothing wrong, per se, with the first example. It contains no ill will and is said with good intent. However, used repeatedly, such phrases lose the meaning they might once have contained. This is why they become platitudes.

The second example is genuine by virtue of being specific. The teacher is referring to something real and tangible which happened during the lesson. By praising Yolande for the determination she showed, the teacher is both indicating that this aspect of her behaviour is good and should be repeated, and that they noticed this and want to make a point of saying that it was good.

Consistently delivering praise of this type – genuine by virtue of being specific – will allow you to maximise the benefits which flow from using praise, both in terms of behaviour and in terms of the learning which follows. Avoiding the perception of insincerity is as important as avoiding insincerity itself.

Reinforcing Positive Behaviour

In terms of using praise to reinforce positive behaviour, here are five techniques you can employ:

- At the start of the year, consistently praise as many students as possible for the various behaviours they demonstrate which meet your expectations. This helps you to quickly and positively familiarise students with the norms and values of your classroom at the same time as it paints a praised-based picture for them of the role of student in your lessons.

- At the start of an activity, praise the behaviour of students who are successfully following your instructions. Draw other students' attention to this and then encourage them to copy what they see. Praise them when they do. This technique can be used with any activity though can lose some impact if overused. To mitigate this potential failing, consider mixing up verbal and non-verbal praise in regard to student behaviour (a thumbs up sign is an effective alternative to verbalising the same praise over and over).

- If a student behaves in a way which runs counter to your expectations, ask them to stop and to change their behaviour. If and when they do this, praise their actions. This includes the decision they made to act differently as well as the behaviour it precipitated. Doing this is a powerful technique for highlighting the varying consequences different behaviours elicit.

- If a group or the whole class conduct themselves in a positive manner through the course of an activity or lesson, feel free to praise students en masse. This praise should still be specific (indicating what it is about their behaviour which has been good) but it can be given at the same time to all the students involved. Personally, I like to praise my classes as a whole group at the end of every lesson in which they have worked well. This helps to end the lesson on a positive note and also acts to bind the class together as a team working towards a common goal.

- When you want all the students in your class to start doing something, try praising and drawing attention to those students who are already doing this. For example, if you want all students to put their bags on the floor and begin the starter activity, praise the students who have already done this. You can then deliver praise to students who follow the positive example. Soon, the majority of the class, if not all, will have done what you wanted and received praise as a result.

Praising Processes

Processes are the things students do rather than the things they create. They are inherent to students rather than external. Effort is a process, an essay is a product. The former is part of who the student is, the latter is something they have created but which then sits externally to them.

Processes persist across lessons, products come and go.

If we praise products, we find ourselves praising the things which are external to students and which are left behind come next lesson. If we praise processes, we find ourselves praising the things which are a part of students and on which they will call in all subsequent lessons.

Here is an example:

A) Wonderful piece of work, Darryl. I love the way the different colours work together.

B) Great work, Darryl, I love the way you have thought carefully about how the different colours can work together.

Notice how the second example talks about the process Darryl has used to produce the work. This is part of his thinking – something which constitutes him as a person and on which he will call again in the future. In the first example, the emphasis is on the work. This is now separate to Darryl and, while the praise may be welcome, he will find it difficult to take the point being made and apply it to what he does in the future.

Praising processes means drawing students' attention to the thinking and effort in which they engage and reinforcing this in the light of the results to which it gives rise.

A further benefit of this approach is that it can be applied across the board, with the way in which you praise processes being tailored to the student in question. Thus, you might praise the way in which a student who usually gives up has persisted through the course of a lesson while also praising the way in which a more-able student has applied their critical thinking in order to pull apart a taxing problem.

In both cases the product is put to one side as it is the process which has caused the product to be created; and it is this behaviour we want to see repeated. Our praise reinforces this message.

Public Praise

Giving praise publicly means assigning status to a student and their actions in front of other people. This can often have a powerful effect, with students feeling that their efforts have been openly acknowledged and validated by other members of the school community. With that said, not everybody responds well to public praise. Shy students and students who struggle to accept praise (due to deeper behavioural issues) may recoil when faced with public praise. For this reason, you should take a moment to think before delivering praise which is public. Of course, as soon as you are familiar with your students this will cease to be necessary.

Here are three examples of how and where to give public praise:

- **During a lesson.** Here, we might decide to make a point of praising the efforts and endeavours of a particular student in front of the rest of the class. For example, we might take a couple of minutes at the end of the lesson to single out two or three individuals who have worked especially hard or who have made great progress despite facing setbacks. We might even ask the rest of the class to applaud them, though this will depend on the relationship we have with our students.

- **During an assembly.** Many assemblies include spaces in which students are acknowledged for their various efforts. Taking advantage of such opportunities allows you to praise students you teach in front of a wide audience. This is usually most appropriate if the students in question have gone above and beyond that which is expected of them. This reflects the higher status accorded by assemblies (with a larger number of students and teachers present than in an individual lesson).

- **In front of parents or other teachers.** Sometimes opportunities will arise to praise a student in front of other teachers – a tutor or head of year, for example. Take advantage of these as they are a great opportunity to reward a student for their efforts. Equally good are parents' evenings.

Here, you can praise the endeavours of a student in front of their parents, rewarding all parties involved (the parents experience the reward vicariously) in the process.

Praise Outside Lessons

Another example of public praise involves finding opportunities to praise students around school, when they are not in your lessons. This sees us remaining alive to the potential for delivering praise through the general course of the working day. Here are three examples you can use:

- **Corridors.** If you see a student in the corridor – before school, in between lessons, at lunch time – and you remember they recently did something in your lessons for which praise is warranted, take the opportunity to deliver it. This is an excellent way to build rapport as it demonstrates to students that you have thought about their efforts and view them as an important individual (someone worth thinking about). For example, on your way to a lesson you might pass a student in the corridor and say something along the lines of: 'Ah, Elliott, I read your essay last night and was very impressed at the way in which you tried to balance the arguments.'

- **Duty.** If you have a break or lunch duty to complete, you can use it as an opportunity to praise students. This will further help you to build rapport and will also work to reinforce those behaviours you choose to praise. In this situation you can deliver praise in the manner outlined above, or you can focus your praise on things students are doing at break or lunch time. For example, you might thank a group of students for setting a good example or praise a student who puts their litter in the bin rather than dropping it on the floor.

- **Home time.** The end of the school day is an excellent time at which to deliver praise. Students will go home with it ringing in their ears. You can make a point of walking past the school exit once or twice a week, if time allows, as students are leaving and use the opportunity to deliver praise of the type outlined above. This is also a good chance to build rapport – you can ask students if they have had a good day, inquire as what they are doing in the evening and wish them well as they head home.

Written Praise

Nearly all of what we have said so far concerns verbal praise. Another option open to us is written praise. This will usually be in the form of feedback written in students' books or on student work as part of our marking.

Here are three techniques on which you can call to ensure written praise is effective:

- Use the student's name and highlight specific things in their work which are good, explaining why they are good in the process. This sees us applying our earlier point about praise being genuine and specific. Personalising what you write by using the student's name serves to demonstrate that the comment you are leaving is specific to them (even if you might have written the same points on twenty books!). In addition, by explaining why certain things are good you open up success criteria for students, making it easier for them to understand what good work looks like.

- Give more praise than targets. This is for two reasons. First, the praise you give will motivate students at the same time as it opens up success criteria for them (increasing their chances of being successful in the future). Second, students will be more likely to take on board any developmental comment you provide if this is preceded by examples of what they have done well. A good ratio to stick to is three positive points to one target.

- Focus on processes. This echoes everything we said earlier. I mention it again here because, when we are marking a piece of work, we can easily fall into the trap of giving praise solely about that piece of work, rather than praise which focuses on the processes which led to the work being created and which can be seen through the quality and nature of the work in question.

Non-Verbal Praise

We also mentioned non-verbal praise above, but only in passing. Let us look at it a little further.

This is praise communicated through gestures, facial expressions and body language. It is an excellent supplement to verbal and written praise; another tool in the praise armoury.

Here are five examples of non-verbal praise you can use with your students:

- **Smiling.** Easily overlooked by the stressed, time-poor teacher. Smiling radiates enthusiasm and is a quick and easy way to show students you are happy to be there and that what they are doing is good.

- **Thumbs up**. This is often well used as a subtle indication to a student who is uncertain or looking for some validation. A discreet thumbs up can indicate that they are on the right lines and should continue in this direction.

- **A look of revelation**. If a student makes a great point or does something good yet unexpected, you can react to this with a look of revelation, as if to say: 'wow, I hadn't thought of that.' This is a nice means through which to positively reinforce surprising or innovative behaviour and/or thinking.

- **Nodding to signal affirmation**. When students are asking you something or explaining a point nodding to signal affirmation is a simple way to encourage them to continue with what they are doing.

- **Gestures which complement speech.** Using gestures to complement your speech means you are reinforcing the content of your words through your body language. This makes for a more powerful message, tends to increase the perception of sincerity, and gives students a means through which they can check they have understood what you have said (by comparing what they have decoded to what they see in your body language).

Praising Role Models

Role models provide students with a set of behaviours they can look at, imitate and learn from. In your classroom, students who exhibit positive behaviour can act as role models for other learners or for the class as a whole. Praising these students draws attention to their behaviour and vicariously reinforces the sense that what they are doing is good and ought to be copied. Here are three examples:

- During a group work activity, praise a group who are working well as role models for the rest of the class. Stop the activity and briefly indicate what the exemplar group are doing and how their behaviour is supporting their learning. If appropriate, ask the group to demonstrate some of what they are doing (whether this is possible will depend in large part on the activity). Another option is to visit individual groups and to praise students within those groups as role models of good behaviour to which the rest of the group should look for guidance.

- When a student completes a piece of work and does so through excellent application of relevant processes, praise them as a role model and highlight their efforts. Share the work they have produced with the rest of the class, drawing attention to why it is good. Explain how students could copy or imitate the things the role-model student has done; if you have a visualiser, use this to display the work on your whiteboard.

- If a particular student is struggling to meet your expectations, use another student as a role model to exemplify for them what successful behaviour looks like. Here, praising the second student works to demonstrate to the first student what it is we want them to do. This has the dual benefit of providing an easily-accessible model they can follow alongside a vicarious reinforcement of why changing their behaviour will be a good thing (because it will bring similar praise and approbation).

Praise Hunts

Unfortunately, some students go through much of their school career without ever receiving praise. This is a great shame, not least on the level of what we would like students to take away and remember about how they were treated and spoken to during their time at school.

In addition, we can find students who regularly experience admonishment for their behaviour, but who rarely ever receive a positive acknowledgement for anything they have done.

You can correct this by going on praise hunts. This involves looking at your class and identifying some or all of those students to whom you have not yet given praise (or to whom you have only given a little).

Primed with the knowledge of who these students are, you can look for opportunities to praise their behaviour, their thinking and the processes underpinning the work they produce.

This will be a great thing for the students in question. It will bring forth all the benefits of receiving praise already outlined, but this will be compounded by the fact that, for them, for whatever reason, the experience is less common than we would like.

A classic example is the quiet student who slips under the teacher's radar. Such a student may rarely receive attention of any sort from their teachers, simply because they do not ask for help and rarely appear to need it. Taking a moment to notice students of this type and then acting on our identification of them means giving them the chance to experience praise and the feelings which stem from that.

Another common trope is the student who is regularly admonished for poor behaviour. In this case, we might unintentionally get into the habit of focussing on the rule-breaking this student engages in. But they will also do some things which are good as well. And we should look to praise these! Not only will this give the student access to the positives associated with praise, but so too will it help them to see that we are not labelling them (for more on which, see earlier).

Praising Change

This involves positively reinforcing changes our students make, as individuals, groups or as a whole-class. The great benefit of praising change is that it provides the student or students who have made the change with a clear indication that we think this alteration to be a good thing. This encourages them to sustain the change.

Here are three examples of how this can work:

- A student begins the year struggling to meet our expectations. They frequently challenge the rules we lay down and look for ways to transgress or undermine the norms we want to foster as part of our classroom culture. As a result of this, we apply negative sanctions to demonstrate to the student the consequences of their actions. After a few months of hard work, the student's behaviour greatly improves.

At this point, praise from us centring on the positive changes the student has made can have a major impact. It shows the student we have noticed the effort they have put into altering their behaviour and that we are acknowledging this and reinforcing it in a positive manner.

- A group of students fail to meet our expectations during the first half of a group work activity. We go over and speak to them, explaining how disappointed we are and reaffirming what we expect from them, why we expect this and what the consequences will be if this is not forthcoming (most likely, that they will not be allowed to work together again).

Five minutes later we return to the group and find their behaviour much improved. Praising this change means we are praising the conscious decision members of the group have taken to follow our instructions and alter their behaviour for the better. Decision-making of this type is something we want to promote and reinforce. Praising it will help us to do this.

- We set a student a target which will help them to improve the quality of their work. This target involves the student in question changing a major part of their approach. For example, we might ask a student doing football in PE to look up before they receive the ball and to do this every time someone passes to them, even though they have never previously done it.

Making such a change will be tricky. It will also take time. Praising the change the student makes will encourage them, helping them to keep focussed on the important task of applying their target. In addition, the praise will further reinforce the idea that the new behaviour is good, tying together the initial feedback and the tangible results stemming from implementation.

Praising Effort

We talked earlier about praising processes, outlining why this is such a powerful approach. One of the processes we mentioned was the application of effort. This is something all students can do, regardless of where they are at, what they know, or how highly they are achieving. Further, it is effort that underpins success, and effort which is an absolute prerequisite for sustained success.

Therefore, praising effort is always doing, in and of itself, as well as part of your wider attempts to praise processes.

When praising effort, it is good to draw students' attention to what you are doing and to make clear the link between effort and success. Doing this helps students to see why effort matters as well as the results to which it can give rise.

Some teachers and schools like to make a virtue out of effort by giving and recording specific effort grades. For example, a school might choose to include effort grades on reports, or to make these available electronically to parents three times a year. Such systems can be very effective. Whether or not they suit your style of teaching and behaviour management is another question.

If they do, I would urge you to follow this approach. You can habituate your students into seeing effort as important by raising its status through the provision of effort grades.

If you do not have an affinity with this approach, you can take a more qualitative line. This will see effort becoming a regular focus of the verbal and written praise you provide, as well as the basis for role models you identify and changes you ask students to make (such as setting them the target of applying more effort during the course of group work activities).

Choose the approach that works for you – both have their benefits. As long as you identify and keep to an approach that suits then your students will reap the rewards.

Conclusion: Making Praise Your Business

All the various points outlined above take us to the central proposition that, no matter what you are teaching, who you are teaching or where you are teaching, to manage behaviour effectively and to maximise progress you should aim to make praise your business.

In summary, this means:

- Look for opportunities to praise students you teach, including those students who may otherwise get overlooked.

- Deliver genuine, specific praise which focusses on processes and efforts.

- Make use of verbal, written and non-verbal praise.

- Use praise to reinforce the positive behaviours you want to see – this includes through vicarious reinforcement (where students see other students receiving praise).

- Use praise as a reward to acknowledge the effort and work individuals, groups and the whole-class have put into your lessons and activities.

- Remember that praise is a means through which status can be achieved and acknowledged. Take this into account when looking for opportunities to deliver praise.

- Giving praise does not have to be confined to the classroom. Look for other ways in which you can use praise to build rapport, support your students and help them to achieve highly.

Chapter Six – Eliminating Low-Level Disruption

We move now to look at one of the trickier areas of behaviour management – eliminating low-level disruption. Many teachers find this the hardest nut to crack. It represents the last obstacle, as it were, on the journey to excellent behaviour management. This is because low-level disruption tends to occur in the space between perfect behaviour for learning and poor behaviour for learning.

By this we mean that many students can tend towards low-level disruption, either intentionally or not, without their behaviour deteriorating to the point of being identified as poor. For example, a student may be largely on task during the course of the lesson, only to spend the last ten minutes trying to chat surreptitiously to the person in front of them while their work is left on the back-burner. Or, another student may wait until they feel the teacher cannot see them and then decide to slide their work to one side while they doodle in their planner.

Such examples of behaviour are common enough. They are neither particularly surprising nor particularly bad. But, the fact remains that they involve students losing focus and prioritising things other than their learning. This goes against your attempts to cultivate the classroom culture you want and also reduces the amount of progress students are likely to make.

When it comes to both these things – creating a culture and maximising progress – accumulation is key. We need to accumulate more and more marginal gains every lesson. Through this, we come to achieve our wider goal and draw students' focus more and more in the direction we want.

Eliminating low-level disruption matters, then. Both for us and for our students: in terms of the culture we want to create and the learning we want to happen. In the remainder of the chapter we will first define and analyse low-level disruption before going on to examine a range of strategies you can employ to reduce and eliminate it.

What is Low-Level Disruption?

Low-level disruption is anything students do which distracts them and/or others from their learning and which is not significant enough to be described as a major behavioural issue.

It includes things such as:

- Social chat

- Talking unnecessarily

- Calling out

- Not starting work or following instructions

- Being slow to start work or follow instructions

- Showing a lack of respect to peers

- Showing a lack of respect to the teacher and/or other members of staff

- Using or trying to use a mobile phone without permission

- Leaving a seat without permission

- Passing notes

- Trying to communicate across the room

- Talking while the teacher is speaking

- Undermining activities (particularly common during group work)

The first thing to say about this list is that maybe we don't want to view it as low-level disruption. Perhaps thinking of it in this way is part of the problem. Instead of calling the collected behaviours outlined above 'low-level' we should simply jettison the modifier and call them disruptions.

This challenges the view that there are different degrees of disruption in the classroom. It does so, not by suggesting a false equivalence between a student shouting and swearing and a student whispering to the person next to them. Instead, it aims to suggest that anything other than learning-focussed behaviour is not what we want. That it is disruptive to the lesson and to the wider aims of the teacher, the class and the school.

Thus, while there are different degrees of disruption, with these being more or less serious, all forms of disruption share the same core aspect: they detract from learning.

Thinking in this way allows us to reframe low-level disruption as unacceptable. It is unacceptable because it stands in the way of learning. To allow it is to accept that learning is not the primary focus for all students at all points in the lesson. Having this rationale to hand gives us a powerful tool to use when looking to eliminate low-level disruption. Students may well question whether such disruption really matters and, as a result, may challenge your attempts to change their behaviour. Formulating your rejoinder on this basis gives you a strong, almost unarguable, position from which to work.

The aim is to be able to demonstrate to students the rationality of your case, using a logic which is very difficult to go against. Here is an example:

Student: It's just a bit of banter, sir. What's the problem with that?

Teacher: Our aim in this classroom is to learn. That's what we're working towards. Anything which takes away from that damages our chances of being successful. We need to use our time as effectively as possible so we can make as much progress as possible. Banter adds nothing and inhibits us from achieving our aims.

While the student may argue back against such a statement, they will struggle to do so coherently. The only way in which they might chip away at the teacher's argument is by attempting to undermine the foundations on which it stands. For example, they may challenge the view that learning is everybody's top priority.

However, taking this approach leaves the student open to the counter-argument that they are happy to disrupt learning rather than focus on it. If true, the student has given their attitude away and undermined their initial justification that there is no problem with a bit of banter. If false, the student will find themselves struggling to maintain their position because they do not really believe in it.

The purpose of the above is twofold.

First, reconceptualising all off-task behaviour as detrimental to learning provides a clear means through which to challenge its manifestation in the classroom. Second, using reason to justify the fact that students need to alter their behaviour provides an excellent model for imitation at the same time as it makes continued counter-argument difficult.

Communicating High Expectations

This takes us onto our first practical strategy for eliminating low-level disruption: communicating high expectations. We are revisiting old ground, based on what we have thought about already in the course of the book.

High expectations demonstrate to students that low-level disruption is not acceptable. They do this by stressing the primacy of learning within the classroom and by indicating that any behaviour which comes into conflict with this value is problematic. Here are three specific ways you can communicate high expectations in relation to low-level disruption:

- Draw attention to low-level disruption before it happens. At the start of the year, talk about what it is, what it looks like and why it is unacceptable. This both communicates the high expectations you have about how students should behave and also sees you tackling the problem prior to it arising. This is not to say that it won't then come about. Just that, if it does, you will have already laid the foundations for dealing with it.

- From the first time you meet a class, ask for silence and then wait. This might be uncomfortable at first. You might need to wait for a few minutes. But doing this will very clearly set out your expectations for behaviour. Subsequently, getting students to be quiet will be easier. This will give you greater authority with which to challenge any unnecessary talking, calling out or social chat.

- Draw a distinction for your students between behaviour which adds to learning and behaviour which detracts from it. You could do this as an activity, with students working in pairs to fill up two sides of a table, with each half referring to one of the categories. The aim here is to make students aware of how you intend to categorise behaviour in the classroom and the means by which you will look at and judge what happens in lessons. You will be able to call on the categorisation in future, indicating to students who engage in low-level disruption that their actions fall into the category of behaviour which detracts from learning.

Not Letting Anything Go

A specific aspect of communicating high expectations involves you working from the premise that, from day one, you will not let anything go in your classroom. This means picking students up on minor transgressions and seemingly small incidences of low-level disruption.

So, for example, in your third lesson with a class you might notice that some students have started to wait a minute or two before beginning the tasks you set. You would then follow up on this immediately, calling attention to the behaviour and asking for a change.

This does two things. First, it shows the students in question that you have seen the behaviour in which they are engaging and that you are not prepared to let them slip below the standards of which you know them capable. Second, it indicates that you expect all students to remain focussed on learning at all times, in everything they do. This point runs deep as the implicit message is that small disruptions will not be accepted, meaning bigger ones are an absolute no-no as well.

Of course, getting the balance right is tricky. Not letting anything go, while an admirable strategy which will serve you and your students well in the long-run, carries with it the risk that you will come over as petty or officious. If this happens, students may grow frustrated. They may also come to develop negative connotations with your lessons.

The solution involves two contrasting elements. When picking students up on small transgressions, do so in a positive and upbeat way while at the same time remaining assertive:

'Steven, you need to begin your work as soon as I ask, thanks. That's what I expect of all the students in my class. It's what I know all of them can do.'

This helps to gild the interaction, making it a more comfortable experience and allowing you to sustain rapport while also changing behaviour that you don't want.

In addition to this, you should look to use praise to reward students for showing learning-focussed behaviour and for changing their behaviour as and when you ask. This acts as a positive counterweight to you picking up on what, to students, might initially feel like trivial matters.

Challenging Disruption

Low-level disruption will nearly always continue if it goes unchallenged. This is because the behaviour is the result of motives. And those motives connect to desires which students want to fulfil. For example, a student might want to enjoy the ease and pleasure of chatting to their friend, or they may want to avoid having their thinking challenged. It follows from this that low-level disruption, once it has begun, is likely to continue until students' motives are satisfied. And this satisfaction is unlikely to ever be final (the motive may be satisfied half-way through one lesson, then return in the next).

I mention this to draw attention to the fact that low-level disruption does not occur out of thin air. It has a cause. And that cause is connected to motives, themselves influenced by reasons, sentiments and the like. As with any negative behaviour, if left unchecked, there is no reason to assume the cause will go away of its own accord. It might, or it might not. More likely the latter.

So challenging low-level disruption is essential. This fact underpins the previous two sections. But how to do it? Well, here are five verbal models you can use as part of your own teaching:

- Begin by praising the on-task behaviour of one or more students in the class. Transition from this to asking students to stop any low-level disruption. This juxtaposes a positive model with the request for behaviour change.

- Praise something positive the student in question has done or is doing, then challenge the disruptive behaviour and ask for change.

- Remind the student why what they are doing is not acceptable and follow this up by giving a concise explanation of what alternative behaviour could look like.

- Use the word 'thanks' instead of 'please.' The former foretells acquiescence while the latter hopes for it. 'Re-focus on the task, thanks, Jim.' 'Can you re-focus on the task, please, Jim?'

- Identify off-task behaviour and, in so doing, remind students of the goal to which the lesson is aiming. As you do this, tie the choice students make to the degree of success they are likely to experience. Finish by indicating the behaviour you want and then waiting to see this.

Applying Sanctions

We have noted elsewhere the importance of defining, communicating and applying sanctions. These are the consequences for poor behaviour.

When it comes to low-level disruption, many teachers shy away from consistently applying sanctions. This is based on the reasonable grounds that to sanction low-level incidents can seem petty or vindictive.

On one level, this makes sense. In the wider world we are wont to let small transgressions go, for the sake of social harmony. So, for example, we may not vocalise our frustration about the communal tea cups never being washed, or we may bite our tongue when a colleague fails to let us get a word in edgeways.

The problem comes when we apply this logic to the social setting of the classroom. There, the demands and expectations of interaction are different. The priority is to maximise learning, rather than to ensure harmony. We want the latter, but we want it in the context of the former, not as an absolute priority or standalone achievement.

As such, sanctions do need to be applied if we want to discourage low-level disruption. If these consequences are not forthcoming, there will be a significantly lower incentive for students to change their behaviour.

At the same time, proportionality is important. Without it, students can rightly claim that the punishment does not fit the crime. On top of this, we will be presenting a model which does not reflect the nature of wider society, and we risk stimulating rancour, as students focus on the perceived injustice they feel they have been dealt.

It is therefore incumbent on us to carefully define the sanctions we will apply for low-level disruption. In so doing we can ensure proportionality, communicate the information to students, and then consistently apply these without fear or favour.

Here is a set of suggestions as to appropriate sanctions you can use to target low-level disruption:

- Non-verbal signals such as frowning, crossed-arms and facial gestures indicating displeasure. These are particularly effective when deployed as soon as you spot any low-level disruption. Over time, students come to associate these with the need to change their behaviour, allowing you to quickly and easily nip problems in the bud.

- Asking students to stay behind at the end of the lesson. This is a sanction in itself but should then be accompanied by a verbalisation of what the student has done wrong, why it was wrong and how you expect them to go about changing their behaviour. A useful technique is to cast the low-level disruption as a third-party separate from you and the student which together you can tackle (this creates a sense that the two of you are working as a team to deal with a shared issue). For example: 'What I saw today wasn't what I know you are capable of. How can we work together to make sure it doesn't come back to our classroom?'

- Verbal disapprobation. This is where we tell the student in question why their behaviour does not meet our expectations. It is important to critique the behaviour rather than the student. Doing this avoids labelling, helps you to maintain rapport and gives the student the opportunity to change how they are acting (much harder to achieve if your language implies that they are somehow a problem).

- Removing privileges directly connected to the low-level disruption. For example, if a student consistently disrupts group work by trying to send their peers off-task, then deny them the privilege of taking part in group work for one lesson. This approach serves to tie the unwanted behaviour to the privilege which behaving positively gives rise to. Students thus see an immediate, tangible consequence for their actions.

Language: Key Phrases

Above, we noted the usefulness of replacing 'please' with 'thanks' in the statements you make to students about their behaviour. A number of other linguistic tools can be called on to subtly support your efforts to eliminate low-level disruption:

- Talking in terms of 'we'. Doing this helps to reinforce the idea that you and your students are part of the same team, working towards the same goal. This might lead us to say 'We're going to re-focus on the task immediately, thanks,' rather than 'You need to re-focus on the task immediately, thanks.'

The first formulation can feel somewhat contrived, however, repeatedly talking in terms of 'we' helps to habituate students into thinking about the class as a unit pursuing a shared objective (this raises the perceived costs of unwanted behaviour).

- Outlining a proposed future. This is where we say something like: 'In the remainder of the lesson we're going to focus all our energies on our learning. This will mean no talking about other things and no slipping into bad habits.' Here, we are presenting students with an articulation of what we want the future to be like. This implants the idea in students' minds and gives something concrete against which they can judge their own behaviour.

- Reframing student expectations. For example: 'This isn't the kind of behaviour I know you're capable of,' or, 'You know that you can keep focussed for a good deal longer. Show me what you can do.' This sees us using our words to undermine low expectations students might have about themselves. Turning matters around like this helps to encourage improved behaviour.

- Unanswerable questions. This tactic can backfire, so use with care. It involves asking students questions which simply can't be answered except through a change of behaviour. For example:

A) Is that how an excellent student should behave?

B) Wouldn't you prefer for me to see you behaving excellently?

C) I thought you could be a role model for us today. You can be, can't you?

I'm sure you can see how these could go wrong. They aim to make students think about the consequences of their actions at the same time as positing a preferable alternative for which praise would undoubtedly be forthcoming. If used in the right circumstances, they can lead to swift alterations in behaviour.

Making Learning Everybody's Business

By doing this, we encourage all students to see the learning which happens in the classroom as partly contingent on what they do. This means we make them feel responsible for the learning – that it is their business. Creating this sense of responsibility gives students a reason not to engage in low-level disruption. It also makes it less likely that they will fall into unwanted behaviour patterns without first thinking about the consequences of what they are considering doing. This is because the idea that they are responsible for what happens in the classroom will be lodged in their minds, acting as a ballast against negative behaviour.

Here are three simple strategies you can employ to achieve this:

- At the start of the lesson, introduce the learning objective and ask students to copy this down. Next, invite them to discuss with their partner what three things they could do to help ensure everybody in the class achieves the objective. Then, ask them to make a note of their three points. Finally, choose a couple of pairs to share their ideas with the rest of the class.

This process helps students to see meeting the learning objective as the goal of the lesson. It also reinforces the idea that their behaviour has an influence on everybody's chances of being successful. In addition, it sees students making a commitment as to what they will do to support learning through the course of the lesson.

- Before your lesson, identify one of the values which underpins the classroom culture you are seeking to create. Start the lesson by reminding students of this value and explaining why it is so important. Then, challenge students to work with a partner to list five different things they could do in the lesson to meet this value. Next, ask pairs to swap their answers with another pair. Finally, ask three students to share one idea with the whole class.

This method is similar to the previous one except here your values are the focus. Again, it concentrates student minds on the idea that learning is their business and asks them to socially commit to this idea through the discussion and sharing of ideas.

- Develop a reward scheme which benefits the whole class but which relies on every student contributing. For example, you might say that you will include a (relevant and exciting) video in the next lesson if the class as a whole can refrain from engaging in any low-level disruptive behaviour. Specify what you mean by this behaviour and then indicate that the whole class have three strikes. If the three strikes are used up, the reward will not be forthcoming.

This can go one of two ways. On the on hand, students buy into the idea and start to watch each other's behaviour as well as their own. On the other hand, one or two students choose not to engage and quickly use up the strikes, leading to disappointment all round. Whether you use the method or not will depend on the type of characters you have in your class and the extent to which you feel they will work positively with the approach.

Always Provide a Choice

Low-level disruption can be frustrating for the teacher. In these situations, the emotions which frustration engenders can influence our decision-making process. This most commonly manifests itself in us issuing ultimatums to those students who have caused us to lose our cool (usually at the point when we feel most frazzled and their behaviour seems like a provocation).

While such reactions are understandable, it is not in our best interests to act this way.

With that said, when the heat is on, it can be hard to remember that the frustration you are feeling is an emotional reaction which you have the power to temper.

An excellent habit to get into is that of always providing a choice for students whose behaviour is not as you expect. Doing this has a few benefits. First, it helps you avoid reacting emotionally (as laid out above) because you need to stop and think, albeit briefly, to define the choice you intend to present. Second, it gives students a way out, offering them a positive alternative to carrying on with any negative behaviour. Third, it avoids ultimatums which raise the stakes between teacher and student ('who will break?' is the question always implicit in an ultimatum), making it more likely that the behavioural problem will be quickly and positively resolved.

Here is an example of what always giving a choice looks like:

'You have two choices, Sara. You can continue to call out while I am talking, in which case I will have to speak to you after the lesson, or you can choose to be respectful and let me speak without being interrupted.'

Or:

'Sam, it's up to you here. Either you choose to start your work when I ask, or you're choosing to go against my instructions and putting the learning second. What do you think is the best thing to do?'

In these examples we see how the student is being empowered through the provision of choice. This gives them a way out, gives them the opportunity to show you they can do the right thing (and receive praise as a result) and stresses the fact that actions have consequences with these being a direct result of the decisions we make.

Habituating yourself into the process of always giving choices will help you to avoid unconstructive interactions with students over low-level disruption. It will also allow you to stay in the driving seat and retain your moral authority when challenging this kind of behaviour.

Empowering and Engaging Students

Thought of more widely, empowering students can be considered a complement to the idea of engaging them. In both cases we are seeking to give students agency; making them feel there is meaning and purpose to their actions and that the choices they make can have a positive impact on their experience of the classroom.

On top of the ideas outlined in the previous section, here are three further ways to empower students:

- Ask them to set their own success criteria for what positive behaviour will look like. These can then be used as the basis for stopping or challenging low-level disruption.

- Provide students with regular, achievable targets in the form of developmental comments. This will help them to feel in control of their learning and their progress.

- Ask students to vote on what type of activities they would like you to plan and then use these as the basis of a reward if behaviour is good and low-level disruption eliminated.

And here are five ideas for engaging students (the underlying point being that if students are engaged they are less likely to fall into disruptive behaviour patterns):

- Plan lessons with an increasing level of challenge. This creates a sense of pace which stimulates students intellectually, drawing their focus.

- Connect abstract concepts and ideas to students' own experiences. This helps to contextualise curriculum content, giving it meaning and purpose within the student's worldview.

- Encourage students to make mistakes and to learn from these. This diminishes the fear of failure, helping students to take more risks with their learning, and making it more enjoyable as a result.

- Use a variety of media sources as the basis of lesson materials. Variety tends to create engagement (through our interest in novelty) and students are used to accessing a range of media as part of their lives outside school.

- Use questions as the basis of lessons, activities and in lieu of learning objectives. These foster a sense of enquiry and give students a goal to which their learning is aiming (being able to answer the question at issue).

Eye-Line and Circulating

If you can see low-level disruption then you can deal with it. Students tend to develop an excellent understanding of when they can be seen by the teacher and when they can't. If they are tempted by off-task behaviour and know that the teacher can't see them, then the costs of doing that particular behaviour are diminished.

Imagine we have two students. They both want to talk to the person sat next to them about what they saw on television last night. The first student is in your eye-line whereas the second student isn't. The risks of being caught talking about something irrelevant are high for the first student and low for the second. Hence, the second is more likely to take a chance.

Thinking about your eye-line at all times helps you to stay on top of low-level disruption. Students are discouraged simply by virtue of knowing you can see them. In addition, you can swiftly challenge anything which develops because you are in a position to see it as it begins.

A good tip is to remain at the front of the room until you are confident students are engaged in their work. Another option is to position yourself when circulating so that you can still see all or most of the class. Also, you might like to think about where best to place yourself during particular activities to ensure you can see what is happening and then intervene where necessary.

Some teachers like to stand at the back of the room while students are working. This provides a different perspective, allowing you to survey the big picture even though students can't necessarily see you.

When it comes to circulating, remember that you can use this to discourage students from low-level disruption simply by walking near them. You might then have a quiet word, or you might not need to. In many cases, simply making your presence felt is enough.

Another benefit of circulating is that it allows you to observe the class from different angles. Changing your eye-line in this way gives you access to different information regarding behaviour. For example, you might realise upon circulating that, while stood at the front of the room, you have actually been failing to pay attention to a group of students on the far left of your field of vision. On circulating you see that this has led to some bad habits developing. Armed with this information you can intervene as appropriate.

Finally, it is worth noting that students will soon learn whether or not you are the kind of teacher who makes a point of observing behaviour and who looks out for specific examples of low-level disruption with a view to neutralising these. If you do this regularly from the start of the year, most of your learners who find themselves tempted to chat, go off-topic and all the rest of it will begin to feel that it is not worth giving in to their desires because of the conscientious approach you bring to patrolling the classroom!

Praising Focus

For our last practical strategy we hark back to an idea previously raised: that of praising processes. One of the processes in which we want our students to repeatedly engage is the application of focus to the task in hand. Through focus, students are able to maximise their progress by targeting their efforts to the work we have set them. Further, the mind tends to be more effective when it is concentrated on a single task, rather than split between multiple points of interest.

Low-level disruption is the antithesis of focus.

It indicates that students are unfocussed and it is for this reason, primarily, that we want to remove it from our classrooms.

You can positively reinforce the idea of focussing by praising the behaviour of students and groups (as well as the whole class if appropriate) who consistently apply themselves to the learning you have planned.

This highlights positive behaviour and draws a contrast with the opposite. The light shone on the effects of low-level disruption are all the brighter as a result.

In conclusion we can sum up the issues surrounding low-level disruption as follows:

- Reconceptualise low-level disruption as unacceptable.

- Communicate this message to your students by stressing and reinforcing your high expectations.

- Look for low-level disruption and challenge it as soon as you see it. Do so positively and assertively, giving students the opportunity to choose how they will improve their behaviour.

- Identify, define and apply sanctions where appropriate.

- Empower and engage students so that low-level disruption becomes a less attractive option.

- Modify your language so that it supports your wider aims of securing good behaviour.

- Praise and reward good behaviour, including focussing on the work and choosing to change from negative to positive actions.

Chapter Seven – Creating Engagement

In the previous chapter we touched on the importance of creating engagement, thinking about how this can help us to eliminate low-level disruption. The topic warrants more attention than this, however. It is worthy of separate treatment because of the central role it plays in creating a positive, purposeful atmosphere in your classroom.

When it comes to creating engagement, we are talking about ways in which you can bind students into your lessons, making them feel a part of what is going on and motivated to pursue the learning objectives you plan. Engagement helps create good behaviour by giving students a sense of meaning. The lesson accords with their motives, rather than conflicting with them.

This means they feel positively predisposed to you, to what is happening and to what you are asking them to do. The result is greater focus and an attitude which fits with the classroom culture you want to cultivate.

Engagement can also be thought of in contrast to its opposite – disengagement. Doing so helps to further illuminate the nature of the former. Disengagement sees students detaching themselves from the lesson and the learning; making an active decision to psychologically remove themselves from what is happening and what you are asking them to do (usually accompanied by a physical signification of this through body language and facial expressions). Engagement, on the other hand, sees the opposite, with students making the decision to actively take part in the lesson and the learning, with this choice being reflected in what they do and say.

In the remainder of this chapter we will first pursue our analysis of why engagement matters, before going on to examine a range of practical strategies you can employ to make it a feature of your teaching.

Why Engagement Matters

There are many possible answers to the question of why engagement matters. Of these, I would suggest three are of most importance. These are:

- Because it creates meaning for students.

- Because it helps students to focus their efforts effectively.

- Because it creates an environment which is inherently better than the opposite.

Let us look briefly at each in turn.

Meaning is important. Without it we can feel lost, alienated and disaffected. Such feelings are uncomfortable. We do not wish them on ourselves and we do not wish them on others. The feeling of alienation is, unfortunately, more common than we would hope in many schools. It is often apparent in students who do not believe the curriculum and what their teachers ask them to do has any purpose in the context of their lives. It can also stem from a sense of failure or the inability to achieve status within the remit of what schools and lessons allow.

Being able to effectively focus your efforts is also important. If we cannot do this then we find ourselves frustrated – in an emotional sense, in relation to goals we are seeking to achieve, or both. Having to split our energies between multiple tasks at the same time decreases the efficacy of our efforts. So does not being able to bring ourselves to put all our focus into the matter in hand. This, in turn, lessens our chances of success, reinforcing a negative-feedback spiral which often leads to an increasing lack of effort based on the perceived futility of working hard.

Engagement can alleviate both these problems. In the first case, it provides meaning through tying the learning to something students view as important. This could be an intrinsic motivator such as wanting to see themselves do better than they have done already or an extrinsic motivator such as the possibility of achieving a good grade.

In the second case, engagement increases focus because it holds and directs student attention. This is for the simple reason that if we are engaged by something then we have a reason for attending to it. In this sense, engagement can be its own reward; a self-fulfilling prophecy which sees us working hard because we are engaged and then reaping the benefits of this through a positive-feedback loop.

This leaves us with our final answer, that engagement creates an environment which is inherently better than the opposite. This argument rests on the fact that we value different things in life. And, in general, all of us value positive experiences which contribute to the growth and wellbeing of ourselves and other people. For this reason, it is self-evident that engagement is preferable to its opposite. Only through engagement can we ensure a higher likelihood of a compelling, positive classroom experience.

Starting with Prior Knowledge

If we begin with prior knowledge we are giving students an opportunity to contextualise their learning within the bounds of their existing knowledge and understanding. This gives them a route through which to access new ideas and information, improving the chances they will be successful at doing this and that they will see what relevance the learning has to their lives and to the world in which they live.

Here are three ways in which to use prior knowledge as a starting point:

- Begin a new topic with a general discussion activity in which students explore what they already know about the topic, or about areas of knowledge connected to the topic. This will give you an opportunity to assess the extent of students' prior learning. You can then use this information to inform your lesson planning. It will also help students to see what follows in the context of their discussions, priming them to make connections between what they already know and that to which you introduce them.

- At the start of a unit of work, introduce the general topic and then invite students to identify three questions they could ask their peers to find out what they already know about this. When the questions have been formulated, ask students to walk around the room and interview 3-5 of their peers. This will prompt discussion of relevant prior learning. It will also give students access to information connected to the topic which their peers possess.

- At the start of a lesson, introduce students to the topic of study and provide three pieces of relevant information. Next, ask students to work with a partner to connect each piece of information to three things they already know. When sufficient time has passed, ask pairs to get into groups of four and share their ideas. Conclude the activity by asking 2-3 groups to share their answers with the whole class.

Stimulating Starter Activities

The start of the lesson is a vital time for creating engagement. If we can grab students here and focus their full attention on learning, maintaining engagement for the rest of the lesson will be much easier.

Here are five examples of stimulating starter activities you can use to do this:

- Hand each student a slip of paper as they enter the room. Half should have questions written on them, half should contain answers. Challenge the class as a whole to match the questions to the answers and then to predict what the lesson will be about.

- Place envelopes on student desks marked with the words 'secret mission.' Inside, there should be a set of instructions telling students what they need to do for the starter activity.

- Display a question or task on the board alongside a countdown timer set to a short period such as two or three minutes. Start the timer immediately and implore students to complete the activity as quickly as possible. This creates a sense of pace and excitement from the word go.

- Make a video of yourself delivering instructions for the starter while wearing a costume connected to the topic of study. Play this as students take their seats. You should get a pretty positive response!

- Display the first part of a story on the board. This should connect to the topic of study. Begin reading the story and then, as it comes to a finish, tell students they must pick it up from there and either write or discuss what happens next. This plays on the psychological draw of narrative, using it as a means to hook students into the lesson.

Real-World Context

Many teachers have faced questions similar to the following, usually a good indicator of burgeoning disengagement:

- 'What's the point of this?

- 'Why will I ever need to know this?'

- 'How's this ever going to help me in my life?'

Such questions squarely demonstrate the earlier points we made about motives, the role these play in causing behaviour, and the connection between motives, reasons, emotions and sentiments.

Successfully countering these questions isn't easy. But doing so helps us to engage students in their learning by providing meaning where they previously perceived none.

An excellent way to do this is by outlining the real-world context of the learning on which your lesson centres. This serves to connect the information and ideas to the wider world, giving it meaning in the process. We will not always be able to prove through this that students will indeed come to use what they learn in later life. However, we will be able to demonstrate the value of the lesson content as it relates to the world in which we live.

Through doing this we also make links beyond the walls of the classroom, which many students find engaging. This is because it gives them a sense of life outside school, of the relationship between what is happening in the classroom and the adult world, and because it implicitly acknowledges that what students are doing in school is intended to prepare them for adult life (playing on the desire most children and young adults have to be older, more mature and more independent).

There are many ways in which you can contextualise learning in relation to the real-world. These include:

- Verbal explanations

- Demonstrations

- Videos

- Newspaper articles

- By analysing or explaining real-world problems

- By using contemporary examples

- Case studies (of which more below)

Case Studies

We will examine this teaching technique in more detail because it is such a useful, widely applicable tool through which we can create engagement.

Case studies are narrative-based examples providing concrete exemplification of abstract ideas and complex information. They do this by situating one or both of these within real-world settings (these could be true or fictionalised; if the latter they will still follow the rules of the real-world).

For example, a case study looking at the story of a migrant worker travelling from Poland to the United Kingdom gives concrete exemplification of abstract concepts such as push and pull factors, economic impetus, and the right to free movement within the EU.

This helps engage students because it provides a route through which they can access learning, assimilate new information and be successful. In addition, students are often able to compare and contrast case studies to either their own experiences or to the experiences of other people about whom they know. This helps them to make further connections between their learning and their own lives, once more increasing engagement.

Case studies can be used at any point in the lesson. Useful tips to remember are:

- A clear narrative is helpful as this gives students a story they can latch onto, analyse and remember.

- Supplementary pictures or videos provide further purchase, giving students a different route through which to understand the story in question.

- You can use case studies before or after introducing the complex information and abstract ideas you want students to learn. In the first case, they will be able to contextualise these using the case study. In the second case, they will be able to apply what they have learned to the case study.

Problem-Solving

This is inherently meaningful because it rests on the existence of a clearly defined purpose. Put another way, problems need solving. Trying to solve a problem is the purpose which gives the act meaning.

For example, I could present you with a selection of information and ideas and ask you to learn these. Or, I could present you with the same selection and ask you to use it to solve a problem. In the latter case, the solving of the problem is your purpose. This goal is defined. It calls on our wider experience of problem-solving and what we know this to entail. Coupled with this is the argument that problem-solving is a significant feature of human life for us all; it is something in which we engage every day, to varying extents, and through which we attempt to realise the desires we have in the world in which we live.

Here are five ways you can build problem-solving into your lessons:

- Rephrase learning objectives, lesson outcomes, lesson titles and activity titles as questions students have to try to answer through the course of the lesson.

- Break activities down into a series of key sub-questions. Encourage students to see answering each question in turn as the best way to successfully complete the activity.

- Use the problems which came before discoveries and advances as the focus of the learning. For example, when teaching about the discovery of penicillin, you might start by asking students to look at the problem which preceded its discovery – the lack of effective treatment for illness and disease. From here, you and your students can move forward, echoing the problem-solving experience as it played out in reality.

- Assign students the role of investigators, scientists or detectives. Present them with a problem connected to the topic of study alongside the materials they need to solve this. The lesson can develop from here and will inevitably be enquiry-led.

- Set students a series of problems and provide instant feedback on the solutions they develop. This gives them the information they need to use trial and error successfully, allowing them to make rapid progress as a result.

Joint Goals

If our students share our goals, greater engagement is likely to follow. This is because students will perceive that what we are asking them to do is aligned with what they are motivated to achieve. We have mentioned this point a few times. However, here are three further techniques through which you can establish, communicate and use joint goals:

- Invite your students to define what the success criteria will be for a given task. To do this, introduce the task to them, talk through what it will involve and ask them to work in pairs to identify three things they think will be included in any piece of work good enough to be deemed excellent.

When pairs have come up with their ideas, ask for various suggestions and scribe these on the board. When you have six or seven, explain that the class will now vote on which they think are the most important. Tell students they have three votes each and then precede to go through each potential success criterion in turn. When the voting is finished, pick out the three top scorers and rank these according to their popularity. These then form the basis of what success will look like in the task.

- At the start of the year, try to spend 3-5 minutes interviewing every student in your class. Come up with a set of questions you can use which will help you to gain an understanding of what students feel they can do already, what they hope to achieve by the end of the year and what they will do to make this happen. Make a note of the conversations in a booklet or on your computer.

Doing this serves three ends. First, it builds rapport between you and your students, showing them that you are interested in their aims and goals. Second, it gives you a wealth of information about the students in your class – information you can use to inform your lesson planning. Third, during the course of the year you can revisit your notes and use these to remind yourself and your students what you are all working towards.

- At the start of a unit of work, introduce the topic and give students five minutes to discuss what they want to learn about this and what they want to be able to do by the end of it. To scaffold discussions, you might want to present some example ideas students can call on, or a set of categories through which they can think.

When the time is up, give students a piece of paper and ask them to make a note of their aims, and to add their name to this as well. Collect the papers in and take some time after the lesson to look through these. You can use the information to structure your planning, telling students in the next lesson that you have read through their aims and will try to help them achieve these in the lessons which follow.

In the penultimate lesson of the unit, return the pieces of paper to their authors. Invite students to assess the extent to which they have achieved their goals, what they still need to do in the last two lessons and what you can do to help them. Ask them to share this information with you – by telling you as you circulate through the room, by writing it on a mini-whiteboard which they then display, or by committing it to the piece of paper before returning this for you to read.

As you will note, each of these techniques serves to demonstrate to students that your lessons are designed to help them achieve their goals; that you and they are working together to reach the same end. This is motivational and engaging.

Scaffolding and Modelling Success

If students feel they can't access the work you set, or if they feel that success is beyond their grasp, then they are likely to experience disengagement. They will look at what they are being asked to do and, whether this perception is right or wrong, assume there is an unbridgeable gap between where they are and where you want them to be. From here, they will start to think that status cannot be achieved in the classroom through working hard (because why bother if success is out of reach?) and will probably feel alienated as a result.

Scaffolding is the first technique on which we can call to neutralise the problem. This sees us doing things which take students a little way towards completing the task in hand, before leaving them to do the rest of the work themselves.

It involves us helping students to bridge the gap so they perceive learning as accessible and therefore engage with it as we hoped they would.

Scaffolding is anything you do which makes a task that little bit easier for students to access. It includes:

- Providing frames or structures students can apply. For example, writing frames, listening frames and sentence starters.

- Giving students part of the answer, explaining why this is the case, and then encouraging them to get the rest of the answer themselves.

- Explaining and re-explaining to individual students so they understand what is expected of them, what different information and ideas mean and how they can successfully engage with these.

- Asking questions which help students articulate and refine their ideas. This process develops understanding and gives students access to the learning by helping them to think about it in a way they may not have realised was relevant.

- Using exemplar work or a worked example as a model which students can copy, imitate or use as a starting point.

This final idea relates to the wider notion of modelling what success looks like. Here, we are concerned with showing students what it means to be successful in a given task. This can include the provision of exemplar work and annotated examples. It can also involve:

- Visually demonstrating how to complete a task

- Verbally demonstrating how to answer effectively

- Verbally demonstrating how to think effectively

- Showing students examples of how to meet each of the success criteria you set for a particular task

- Asking a student to show their peer how they have gone about engaging with a task or trying to meet the success criteria

In each case, the aim is to give students access to success; to help them understand what they need to do to engage with the learning and achieve their aims.

Challenging All Students

Lessons which offer no sense of challenge are unstimulating. This is because they ask students to simply repeat what they can already do. As such, the sense of progression and development is missing. We lose the benefits which stem from novelty and risk implying that we think little of students' abilities. Unchallenging lessons do not communicate high expectations.

The flipside of this is that if we set out to challenge all our students in every lesson we teach, then we are looking to engage them from start to finish at the same time as we communicate very clearly the high expectations we have concerning their abilities and that of which we think them capable.

Here are three techniques you can use to ensure your lessons are challenging for all students:

- Seek to elicit information about where students are at with their learning. Do this by assessing learning within the lesson. Listen to students, observe them, read their work, ask them questions and use whole-class feedback techniques to elicit information about what they know. You can use this information as a basis from which to challenge students. Knowing where they are at means knowing what will challenge them and what will simply be repetition.

- During activities, circulate through the room and pose questions which are tailored to individual students. These questions should be challenging, provoking the students to whom they are posed to think carefully about the lesson topic. By tailoring your questions you can ensure they meet the needs of different students. Bloom's Taxonomy is a useful framework for this. Another option is to see questions as being on a continuum which runs from concrete to abstract. The more able a learner is, the more abstract the question you pose to challenge them.

- Plan extension tasks and questions for every activity in your lessons. This ensures more-able students remain engaged while other members of the class are working on completing the main activity.

Demonstrating Progress

We assess students regularly, record their attainment and analyse their knowledge and understanding, comparing this to where we want and expect them to be, based on the lessons we plan and teach. It can be difficult for learners to get a similarly accurate sense of the progress they are making.

Students do not view lessons and learning in the same way we do. For them, school is much more like a series of events, one after the other, which, together, form the day, the week, the month, the term and then the year. This continuous experience, coupled with the less mature perceptions of time which children and young adults possess, makes it harder for them to look critically at what they have achieved and to compare this to what they were previously capable of doing.

This can lead to disengagement. If students do not feel like they are making progress, they may be less inclined to work hard, to put in effort and to focus on the learning you ask them to do.

It is therefore beneficial if you have strategies through which you can demonstrate to students the progress they are making. This helps them to gain purchase on the extent to which they are reaching their goals, as well as the idea that the effort they put in does and will bear fruit.

Here are three techniques you can use:

- Track the targets you set students by writing them at the front of their books. Every time they feel they have met a target, ask them to turn to the front and to make a note of the evidence which proves this. When you take their books in to mark, sign off on the evidence to indicate agreement – or ask students to look again at their target and to see if they could do more to successfully meet it.

- On an intermittent basis, lead students in a five-minute reflection. The easiest way is to do this as a plenary. During the reflection, ask students to think about the progress they have made. Focus their thinking by providing a set of questions such as the following:

What do you know now that you didn't know before?

What can you do now that you couldn't do before?

What would you tell your old self about the learning you have done in the last few weeks?

- At the end of every half-term, plan a twenty minute reflection period into the last lesson you have with your class or classes. Use this time to review all the learning which has taken place during the course of the term. Ask students to compare this to where they were at a couple of months previous. Then, invite them to write one to two paragraphs detailing the progress they have made and what they think they need to focus on in the next half-term. As the year progresses, ask students to return to their earlier reflections each time a new review comes around. This will make it increasingly easy for students to visualise the progress they are making.

Active Learning

By active learning I do not mean that all students are stood up, moving around the room. Instead, I mean that students are actively engaged in the task in hand. This is in contrast to passive engagement, where students are able to sit back and let the learning flow over them.

An example of passive learning is a student sitting and listening to the teacher talk without paying attention to what is being said or worrying too much about whether or not they take anything in. An example of active learning is a student reading an article and, as they do, trying to analyse it in the context of their prior learning, making connections to an enquiry question posed by the teacher, and trying to assess whether they agree with what the article puts forward.

I use reading as an example of active learning quite deliberately so as to reinforce the point that this type of learning can come in any form. The key is that students should be actively engaged with what they are doing – attending to this with their full attention.

This type of learning is far more engaging than passive learning. This is for the obvious reason that it does actually engage one's mind (in contrast to passive learning, which doesn't). In addition, though, active learning is inherently more meaningful and purposeful. This is because the student is setting the new information in the context of what they already know and because they are manipulating and using that information in order to achieve one or more ends.

This leads us to the conclusion that planning active learning into your lessons builds engagement. You can do this at every stage of a lesson, no matter what activities you are using.

Variety

Our final practical suggestion when it comes to creating engagement is to include variety in your planning. As we have said elsewhere, novelty tends to naturally stimulate human beings and, in so doing, causes us to engage with whatever is in front of us. It is for this reason (in part) that advertisers and marketers produce new promotional materials and why companies bring out new products, even if they may be largely similar to what came before.

When planning your lessons – and particularly when planning a unit or scheme of work – ask yourself whether you are including a sufficiently varied set of activities and tasks. If you are, engagement is more likely to follow.

And with that we conclude this section of the book. Let me finish by providing a summary of the points made above:

- Engagement is motivational. It gives students purpose and nearly always leads to better behaviour.

- Disengaged students tend to withdraw from learning physically and psychologically. They may also look to gain status within the classroom through other means.

- If you make creating engagement a focus of your planning and teaching you are likely to stimulate excellent behaviour.

- Engagement can be encouraged by contextualising learning, either in relation to the real-world or to prior experience.

- Ensuring all students are sufficiently challenged and finding ways to help students to be successful is also good.

- As is the creation and communication of joint goals.

- Finally, you can help students to learn actively by ensuring your lessons do not allow them to remain passive; variety is one route to achieving this, as is stimulating student endeavour by helping them to visualise the progress they have made.

Chapter Eight – Building Rapport

Building rapport sits neatly with creating engagement. While in the last chapter we thought about specific things you can do to motivate students and bind them into your lessons, here we will look at strategies and techniques you can employ to develop good relationships with them. These are usually the basis of effective behaviour management over time. Teachers who have positive, learning-focussed classrooms tend to have good relationships with their students.

This doesn't mean they try to be friends with their students. The rule is always friendly but not friends. Nor does it mean these teachers avoid tough decisions, enforcing sanctions or asking students to work hard even if they don't want to. Far from it.

Teachers who develop good relationships with their students demonstrate through their actions – the planning, teaching and assessment in which they engage – that they have their students' best interests at heart and that it is through this prism they make decisions. This builds rapport as much as being friendly does; we all feel positively disposed towards people if we feel they have our interests at heart.

In this chapter, then, we will look at how to build rapport, starting off with a brief consideration of just what rapport actually is – and why it matters – before going on to look at practical strategies and techniques.

What is Rapport?

Rapport is the affinity we have with one another. It refers to a harmonious relationship; one in which both members understand each other's feelings or ideas. Rapport rests on good communication. If we have a relationship characterised by bad rapport, it is likely that the communication taking place within that relationship will leave something to be desired. One or both sides will be failing in their efforts to connect.

Good rapport means we understand one another. As part of this we will most probably trust one another as well. Seeing as how the relationship we have developed is harmonious, we will operate under the assumption that our interests are aligned and that we are motivated to work in support of one another, if not in total then at least in part, and certainly for the duration of the time we are together.

In the classroom, rapport manifests itself as a shared understanding between you and your students. This understanding encompasses the idea that you are working together in pursuit of the same end – student success. That success may be defined precisely, such as in terms of exam results, or it may be defined more widely, such as in terms of learning about a subject, enjoying being in the classroom and, as a result, feeling productive and creative.

We can all recognise rapport when we see it. There are usually smiles, mirrored gestures and a sense of ease and relaxation emanating from people's body language. This reflects the fact that rapport helps us to feel at one with the situation in which we find ourselves. This feeling, in turn, dispels uncertainty and any sense of conflict, or potential conflict, putting us into a comfort zone within which we can feel calm.

Rapport does not happen immediately. It takes time to develop. What is more, and as in any relationship, to be sustained, rapport must be attended to on a regular basis. We cannot assume that, once it arrives, it will remain as it is without a degree of effort and maintenance on our part.

While there are some ways in which we can speed up the process of building rapport, the fact stands that the best general route to its development is the expression of genuine sentiment. By this I mean that it is very difficult (though not impossible) to foster rapport without a sense that you are truly interested in the wellbeing and goals of your students. Ultimately, good relationships tend to rest on a foundation of mutual respect and concern, with this stemming from a belief common to those involved that both parties have inherent value and are important.

Why Does Rapport Matter?

Without rapport, behaviour management becomes much harder. We do not have the sense of harmony and shared endeavour we would wish for, meaning the attempts we make to communicate our classroom culture are more likely to fall on deaf ears. Furthermore, the interactions we have in the classroom are not gilded by the belief that we are all in this together, working towards a shared goal. This serves to militate against our students reading our intentions as positive. So too does it make it harder for us to develop the shared norms and values we want.

In a classroom characterised by a lack of rapport, communication between teacher and students will suffer. There may be more misunderstandings, a less positive atmosphere, and a sense that people are pulling in different directions. Most probably, there will also be a lack of trust, with students reluctant to take the teacher's word at face value and to accept that the things they ask them to do have their best interests at heart.

In contrast, a classroom in which there is good rapport will always be more productive. This has the consequence of improving progress and achievement for the students involved, as well as providing them with a more enjoyable and fulfilling experience.

It is not just that rapport creates relationships in which we feel safer, more comfortable and more at home. It is also that we achieve a series of cumulative gains which help us to maximise learning and develop the best classroom environment possible.

For example, if we have a good rapport with our students then every time we ask them to change their behaviour, to complete a task or to think about a question, the request is met with acquiescence and good humour. This compares favourably to a situation in which we have little or no rapport with them. In the latter case, we encounter refusals; our requests are questioned; and, while students may engage with what we ask them to do, they will tend to do so to a far lesser extent.

Over the course of a single lesson, good rapport save us a considerable amount of time and energy. Over the course of a term or a year, this adds up to a significant amount of additional learning.

Finally, let us just reiterate that, while good rapport is beneficial for our students in the context of their achievement, it also remains an excellent route through which to ensure our lessons are generally more enjoyable than they would otherwise be. And this applies to our experience of them as well as our students' experiences.

It is much more enjoyable, from a teaching perspective, to work with a class with whom we get on well. This makes us positively disposed to the experience, causing us to look forward to it. The same is true of our students. If they anticipate a good lesson, they are more likely to experience one. So too us. Rapport is central to achieving this.

Communication in all its Forms

So how do we go about building rapport?

The first thing to consider is how you communicate while teaching. Remember that everything you do and say sends a message to your students. Your voice, body language, how you dress, how you carry yourself, the words you say and the lessons you plan: all of these give students information to decode and assimilate.

This information forms the basis of students' perceptions about you. And it is these perceptions which influence the relationship you and they are able to establish.

Knowing this, it becomes apparent that you can build rapport during every part of your teaching. By attending to the kind of messages you send out, you can shape and mould these messages so they aid the development of good relationships.

For example, you can plan lessons which are well-organised, challenging and which clearly demonstrate an understanding of where students are already at with their learning. This conveys a powerful message about your professionalism, as well as a secondary message concerning your attention to detail when it comes to assessing student progress and using this information to benefit everybody in the class.

Another example is turning up on time. Ridiculous, I know! Such a simple thing. Yet on countless occasions I have seen teachers arrive late to a lesson (through tardiness rather than circumstances beyond their control) and then wonder why they struggle to develop a sustained positive relationship with their students. They fail to understand that arriving late sends a message – whether intended or not – which students identify, take on board and remember.

The first way in which you can look to build rapport, then, is to pay attention to all of the communication in which you engage and to ensure that the messages you send are both consistent and reflective of the classroom culture you want to develop.

Positivity and Enthusiasm

Nearly all of us prefer positivity to negativity. On top of this, enthusiasm is infectious. If we radiate both of these every time we step into the classroom, then we go a long way towards building excellent rapport with our students.

Positivity brings with it a sense of purpose. If we operate from a positive mindset then we are suggesting that the process of being in the classroom is good in and of itself. This contrasts to the mindset of negativity, which works from the premise that the classroom does not represent something good, but something to be critiqued.

I am not suggesting a Panglossian approach is to be preferred, through which we ignore all evidence of things which need improving and work under the assumption that everything is for the best in the best of all possible worlds.

Rather, I am providing a rationale as to why positivity has a good effect – sometimes a profound effect – on the rapport we establish with our classes. Put simply, we prefer to be around positive people. They give us energy, convey a sense of purpose and stimulate an upbeat atmosphere.

When it comes to enthusiasm, we must again caveat the point by indicating that excessive or feigned enthusiasm can actually work against building good relationships. In both these cases a question arises in students' minds about whether or not what they are seeing is genuine. And if there is a question mark over the truth of what one is perceiving, then that which is being seen ceases to have the same level of impact.

But, in general, being enthusiastic serves an important purpose. It conveys to students the message that you are happy to be in the classroom with them, that you think what you and they are doing together is engaging and interesting, and that you believe there is meaning to the lesson as a whole.

Teachers who display no enthusiasm are not as enjoyable to learn with. Of course, learning does not have to be enjoyable – sometimes it is simply a matter of getting on with the hard work we have in front of us, however boring this might seem. Yet, we can all remember those teachers who displayed enthusiasm when they taught us – whereas those that didn't shine far less bright in our memories.

Enthusiasm is not just about high energy and visual displays of excitement. If this does not fit with how you see yourself in the classroom then no problem. Instead, enthusiasm is about displaying interest, particularly in the learning which forms the basis of your lessons. So, for example, we could imagine a very quiet and calm teacher who nonetheless radiates enthusiasm when they talk about the topics they teach. It is the showing of interest which marks out enthusiasm, with that demonstration capable of taking many forms.

Modelling Manners

Enthusiasm and positivity certainly help to oil the wheels of relationships, making it easier for us to work together and get on well in each other's company.

Manners are similar. They have various functions within any culture and society. However, one of these is as a means through which to show the people with whom we are interacting that we have taken account of and are sensitive towards their feelings.

This can be seen in how we feel when someone has treated us with good manners. Such experiences leave us feeling respected and important; they give us a sense of our own worth.

Contrast this with how we feel after experiencing bad manners. We may feel offended, disrespected or put out. This is partly because we think the norms of social interaction have been broken. Partly because we see the behaviour as an affront to our sense of who we are and how we ought to be treated.

All of this leads us to the point that you can build rapport by modelling excellent manners at all times. This will:

- Demonstrate to students that you have taken their feelings into consideration and want to treat these with care.

- Set an example for your class to imitate; one in which showing respect and concern for the feelings of others is a top priority.

- Establish an atmosphere of civility which puts students at ease, helping them to feel safe, secure and able to focus on their learning.

It is worth noting that modelling good manners can include you drawing attention to what you are doing. So, for example, if a group of students are not doing what you asked, you might indicate that you behave differently from this through the manners you model and that you would like them to mimic your approach.

This technique is all about making students actively aware of both the thoughts which underpin good manners and the influence these have on behaviour. Essentially, we are making the implicit explicit.

Greeting Students

Greeting students as they enter your room builds rapport by sending a message that you are pleased to see learners arriving at your lesson. It also provides an opportunity to speak to students as soon as they come into the room, which again helps to foster good relationships.

An additional benefit of this approach is that it helps you to define the classroom as a shared space, but one of which you are in charge. This is achieved through the physical positioning of yourself at the doorway, welcoming students into the shared learning space at the same time as you indicate (through doing the welcoming) that you are leading the lesson.

It is not always possible to greet students at the door, though. For example, you might have two consecutive lessons in different parts of the building. In such a situation your students might arrive at the classroom before you.

An alternative approach is to greet the class as a whole. This sees us standing at the front of the room and welcoming all students into the lesson at the same time. Through doing this, we realise many of the benefits of standing at the door to greet learners, even if it is not possible to do this.

Showing Interest

It goes without saying that a perfunctory greeting through which we show little interest in our students will not have much impact in terms of building rapport. This leads us onto the wider point that showing interest in students is an excellent tool through which to improve our relationships with them.

If we show interest we indicate to the person in question that we think they are important. And we all like to feel important. Being made to feel unimportant – being snubbed or ignored – can be an uncomfortable experience. And we do not tend to seek out and want to repeat experiences of this type.

The converse is also true. If someone shows interest in us – our thoughts and ideas – then we are more likely to want to talk to them again and to view them in a positive light.

Here are five examples of how and where you can show interest:

- When you ask students a question, make sure you wait for their response and demonstrate interest through your body language and the follow-up questions you ask.

- When greeting students, and if appropriate, make specific comments or ask specific questions which demonstrate your interest in them as individuals. For example: 'How did you get on with that homework, Sam?' 'Hi Janine, ready for another good lesson today?' 'Rahul, I've thought about that question from last lesson – remind me to talk to you about it later on.'

- Learn students' names and use these regularly. If you struggle with names, tell students this and ask them to help you.

- During activities, either circulate through the room and engage students in conversations about their work, or call them up to the front one at a time and talk to them there.

- Try to remember pieces of information you elicit about individual students. For example, their hobbies, their interests and their future goals. You can call on this information in the future to help build rapport. Every time you do, you will show the student in question you are interested in them as an individual.

Talking Outside Lessons

We can build rapport outside lessons as well as while we are teaching. Every time we see a student around school it is an opportunity to speak to them and to develop the relationship we have with them.

Something as simple as smiling and saying 'hello' when we chance upon them will have a positive impact. We might take things a step further by chatting to them while we are on break or lunch duty, or by telling them about something connected to their work when we see them before registration.

The aim is to continue with the wider point of showing interest and modelling excellent manners. Through doing this, we continue to demonstrate to students that we think they are important and that we value them as individuals. The memories which result from these brief experiences will be stored in their minds alongside their perceptions about us as a teacher, the lessons we teach and the content of those lessons.

Every time you see a student you teach outside of lessons view it as an opportunity to further establish rapport with them. A friendly word lifts us all up, as does a smile and a recognition that we are there and that we matter.

Playing a Role

Sometimes, if we are struggling to build rapport with a class or an individual student, we might need to take on a role in order to establish better working relationships. This sees us changing the set of behaviours we normally associate with being a teacher and adopting a different set which we feel are more likely to help us achieve our goals in the short-term.

This is not always an easy thing to do. It tends to be necessary on those occasions when our usual methods of building rapport have failed. As such, there is a certain implicit challenge to our sense of self which we must overcome. That challenge goes something like: 'I normally work in this way and manage to build rapport. Why isn't it happening this time? Is there something wrong with me?'

Such self-talk is common, but false. If your usual approach does not work this is a reflection of the efficacy of the approach in a given situation, not on you as an individual. The real question you should be asking is: 'If my usual approach doesn't seem to be working, what other method could I try instead?'

Note how the subject of the two thoughts is different. In the first case, we are the subject. In the second case, the most suitable approach is the subject. This subtle change of focus makes taking on a different role much easier. No longer do we view such a change as an implicit attack on who we are. Rather, it becomes an opportunity to problem-solve by trying something different.

So what does it mean to take on a different role?

Well, for example, we might usually play the role of motivator while we are teaching and find that, for once, this doesn't work, serving to alienate students rather than engage them. Having ascertained this fact, we would then need to look for a different role which might help us to build rapport. Perhaps we try the role of questioner or facilitator and find that one of these works better.

At root, this technique is about coming to appreciate that one size does not always fit all in terms of building rapport. A certain flexibility over the role we play in the classroom gives us the space in which to switch and change our behaviours. The alteration often only needs to be subtle. But through this we can respond to the specific dynamic of a class or the prior experiences of a particular student.

Self-Deprecation and Humour

Self-deprecation sees us playing up our weaknesses and demonstrating the ability to laugh at ourselves. It is engaging because it breaks down the barrier between audience and performer – in this case, students and the teacher. This happens through the tacit acknowledgement that audience and performer both know the rules of the game, and also know how to subvert them to have a little fun.

Humour builds rapport because laughter is infectious, because seeing the comedy in things brings levity and lifts our mood, and because humour is based on a set of shared understandings. With this said, some humour works on the basis of exclusion, with individuals or groups being made the butt of jokes. This type of humour should always be avoided in the classroom as it alienates those who are excluded and implies that creating a hierarchy of different groups within the class is somehow acceptable.

When using humour and self-deprecation, there is a fine line between engaging your students and undermining yourself. Too much humour or self-deprecation may tip the balance of your classroom further in that direction than you would like. If this happens, it will be detrimental to your behaviour management. You will have to exert a great deal of energy to pull matters back to where you want them and will also have to put humour and self-deprecation on the back-burner for a while, perhaps becoming sterner than you would like in the short-term.

Getting the balance right involves carefully judging the mood and dynamic of your class. You can then decide how much humour and self-deprecation is appropriate. As a general rule of thumb, the better you know a class, the easier it is to make this judgement.

To avoid unintentionally giving rise to situations you don't want, start off by keeping humour and self-deprecation to a minimum. Do not exclude it altogether, but do begin by using only a little. This way, you can quickly and easily judge the effects to which it gives rise before using this information to inform future decision-making.

Some classes respond poorly to humour, others well. Knowing this in advance – by first testing the water – will help you to moderate and monitor your use of the technique, allowing you to find a good balance which builds the kind of rapport you want.

Starting and Ending the Lesson Well

Creating a calm and positive atmosphere at the start and end of your lessons builds rapport because students tend to remember these sections of the lesson more vividly than they do other parts. We will look at each in turn.

Starting the lesson well means students enter your room and begin their learning with a sense of purpose and positivity. We can achieve this by greeting them at the door, asking questions, showing interest, being well-prepared, planning an engaging starter through which they can experience success and have their thinking challenged, and by radiating enthusiasm.

This is a summary of things we have already looked at.

The key here is to bring them to bear with the specific intention of building rapport at the start of your lessons; finessing your relationship with students by getting the lesson off on the right foot. This sends students a clear message about your expectations (something else we have looked at) while also encouraging them to expect a continuation of the positive start through the remainder of the session.

Ending the lesson well means students leave with a feeling of positivity. This builds good memories, underpins rapport and presages a likely return to these feelings the next time students see you or come to your lesson. Here are five strategies for ending your lesson well:

- Keep an eye on the time. Begin ending the lesson 3-4 minutes before it is due to finish. This gives you control and prevents chaotic scenes as students try to pack up in a truncated time period.

- Thank the class as a whole before they leave the room. Be specific in your thanks, drawing attention to things the class have done well such as applying themselves and working hard when faced with challenges.

- Praise individual students, focussing on specific processes they exhibited during the course of the lesson.

- Use some humour. It could be a gentle joke or a reference to something which happened during the lesson. Students will take away the positive feeling this engenders as they leave the room.

- Signpost the learning students will do next lesson. As you do, convey your enthusiasm for the upcoming topic and indicate why you think students will find it interesting.

Personalised Feedback

Feedback tells students what they have done well and why this is good, provides the information they need to make improvements, and causes them to think differently to how they might otherwise have thought.

Personalising feedback builds rapport by reinforcing the idea that you think students are important and that you have their best interests at heart. Feedback which is not personalised is more likely to be discarded or ignored. It may also be interpreted (whether rightly or wrongly) as indicative of a lack of care and concern on behalf of the teacher.

It is easy to personalise feedback, whether it is verbal or written. In both cases, using the student's name is the first step. Then, you should look to give feedback which shows you have analysed their work. To do this, read what they have written, listen to what they say or observe what they do and provide a relevant comment or question.

Repeatedly doing this will not only help students to make great progress but will also cultivate in their minds the notion that you are interested in helping them to learn and that, as a result, you pay attention to the work they produce.

Circulating and Supporting

Our final technique for building rapport is circulating and supporting. Earlier, we mentioned that the former may at times need to be combined with you keeping a watchful eye over behaviour in the class. Hopefully, as time progresses and your class come to accept and live up to your high expectations, as well as the norms, values, roles and ways of gaining status which constitute these, you will find it increasingly easy to circulate. As this becomes the case, you will be able to give more of your time over to supporting students.

Doing this will help them to learn. You will be able to give advice and direction, make suggestions and ask questions. All of this will further impress upon them the central fact that you are there to support them and to help them with their learning.

If circulating and supporting proves difficult because you need to spend time watching students and keeping their behaviour focussed, you might like to try the alternative approach of calling students up to the front and talking to them about their work from your desk. This is not ideal, but it does allow you to combine the twin roles of keeping an eye on behaviour and giving individualised support.

As we conclude this chapter it is worth noting that all of the points above are bound by the same theme. Namely, that building rapport in the classroom is about creating a positive atmosphere, showing students you think they are important and showing you want to help them to do well. Your general demeanour can thus also aid you in building rapport, if it carries within it these key messages.

Here is a brief summary of the points we have made:

- Good rapport means having harmonious, positive relationships with your students in which you and they are working towards a shared goal and with a shared understanding.

- Rapport matters because it helps foster a focussed learning environment, makes behaviour management easier and significantly increases the chance that lessons will be successful, that students will learn more and that this learning will be enjoyable.

- Every aspect of your communication conveys messages which can support or work against your attempts to build rapport.

- Treating students as individuals, demonstrating that you think they are important and making it clear that you have an interest in their ideas, wellbeing and success will help you to establish rapport.

- Any strategy you use to try to build rapport will be far more effective if it is underpinned by a genuine desire to establish and maintain good relationships.

Chapter Nine – Common Problems and Scenarios

In this, our penultimate chapter, we turn our attention to common problems and scenarios which can arise during the course of teaching. Everything we have looked at so far will come into play when trying to deal with these issues. Indeed, it will also have a role in preventing them arising in the first place. Nonetheless, it is helpful to have a point of reference to which one can turn in times of difficulties.

The list of problems and scenarios is not exhaustive, but it does cover most of the main issues which can arise in any given class. In each case, I will suggest three solutions. The reasons for this are as follows:

First, not all examples of a problem or scenario will be identical. Therefore, it may be less helpful if I present only one possible solution for dealing with each general case. Second, you will no doubt have your own teaching style, approach to behaviour management and relationship with the class you teach. By providing multiple solutions I hope to give you sufficient information and ideas such that you will be able to mould and adapt these to suit your needs.

Third, and finally, solving behavioural problems is not an exact science. The range of techniques and ideas contained in this book indicate this. I do not want to undermine the case here by implying that specific problems can only be solved in a specific way.

With all that said, let us look at the scenarios alongside some possible solutions.

Refusing to do Work

Explanation: One or more students refuse to do the work you have set.

Solution 1: Try to identify the cause of the problem. Is it that students do not understand the work or do not know how to complete it? Ask probing questions to elicit information about students' understanding of the task. If this is limited, provide them with a model of what successful engagement looks like at the same time as you re-explain what you would like them to do. As part of this, you might also want to assess whether there is any ambiguity in your explanation of the work you want students to complete. If there is, simplify your explanation to make it clearer.

Solution 2: If students are lacking motivation, tie completion of the work to wider goals. For example, you might invoke the current target the student is working towards or their general desire to do well in school and be successful. As part of this, explain to students why what you have asked them to do is in their interests. Couple this with further explanation or modelling of the task. Then, indicate the specific steps you would like students to take to begin. Praise the process they go through when they do this. For example: 'Thank you for listening to my comments and acting on them, it shows maturity and that you can make positive decisions.'

Solution 3: Reiterate your expectations to students, explaining that, in your classroom, completing all the work set is a minimum expectation which everyone must live up to. Tie this to your wider aims of helping students to learn as much as possible and using their time with you productively. As part of this, you might like to make a general comment referring to the engagement shown by other members of the class. As you do, indicate that the student has a choice to live up to this behaviour and imitate it, or to continue refusing to work – with these two choices leading to different consequences. State what the consequences are and invite the student to make a positive choice. If they do, praise their behaviour. If they don't, explain the sanction and tie your application of it to the choice they made.

Seeking Attention

Explanation: One or more students seek to gain your attention or the attention of their peers.

Solution 1: When the class are working on the task you have set, call the student or students who have been trying to gain attention to the front of the class to speak to you. Explain the behaviour you have observed and ask them why they are doing it. If they cannot provide a reason, indicate the behaviour has a negative impact on other people's learning and that, for this reason, it needs to cease. If they do give a reason, assess the value of this. Perhaps they have a genuine need to feel noticed and you can agree to meet this need in a positive way – for example, by going and listening to their ideas at the start of all main activities.

Solution 2: If one or more students try to gain attention while you are talking to the class as a whole, stop what you are doing immediately. Turn to the student or students in question and say something along the lines of: 'Our aim as a class is to learn. I need to lead that learning and I can't do it if you behave in this way. I don't expect it and you know that you can behave better than you are doing. If you continue trying to draw attention away from me, I will ask you to leave the room until I have finished talking to the class.' Here we are assertively reinforcing our expectations, drawing a link between the interruptions and the learning of the class as a whole, and also stressing that behaviour leads to consequences.

Solution 3: Some students find it really difficult to control their desire to draw attention. In these cases, it is often good to work with the student to develop a technique they can use. This is about you and them identifying the behaviour which inhibits learning and working together to eliminate or minimise it. Call the student or students aside, maybe even talk to them outside the room, and explain you have observed their behaviour and that it is not acceptable. Ask what you and they can do to change it. From here, you can develop a strategy together, such as counting to ten before speaking, non-verbal signalling or the student writing down thoughts and ideas which you then look at when the class as a whole are working.

Disrupting Others

Explanation: A student seeks to disrupt either the class as a whole, the people sat near them, or the group with whom they are working.

Solution 1: Try to identify the cause of the disruption. If it is a regular behaviour pattern, the student in question may think this behaviour is acceptable or may have an attitude toward your lesson which needs modifying. If it is a seemingly random occurrence, the student in question might be having a bad day, be over-stimulated after lunch or have some problem with accessing the work. Having identified the cause of the disruption (by talking to the student in question) you will be well placed to deal with it. As part of this, you might choose to ask the student how they would deal with it if they were in your shoes.

Solution 2: Isolate the student in question by asking them to move somewhere in the classroom where they can work on their own. This could even be to your desk, or to a spare space next to your desk. As you do this, be sure to explain your actions and to tie the sanction you are applying to the behaviour in which the student has engaged. Stress the primacy of learning and the fact that you cannot accept behaviour which goes against this. Indicate the student now has an opportunity to make a positive choice and change their behaviour. Make sure they can access the work before leaving them – it is important to demonstrate that sanctioning their behaviour does not make you any less likely to help and support them with their learning (and this sends a powerful message about your desire to work in their best interests).

Solution 3: If the disruption comes during paired or group work, explain to the student that you have certain expectations about how learners should behave while taking part in this. Stress that you use such activities because of the benefits they bring in terms of learning. Indicate what behaviour you would like to see from the student in question and say why this is important, as well as why it will help them, you and others. Be clear that the student now has a choice: to change their behaviour based on what you have said, or to continue. Tell them that if they opt to continue, the consequence will be that they do not take part in paired or group work for the time being. If they change their behaviour, be sure to praise the process. If they do not, follow through on the sanction.

Challenging Your Authority

Explanation: A student challenges your authority. This could be in response to a request, the application of a sanction or through the breaking of class, school or societal norms.

Solution 1: If a student challenges your authority in front of the whole class, try to avoid turning this into a stand-off in which one of you has to back down. This usually escalates the situation and causes further problems. Address the behaviour rather than the student, stating why it is inappropriate and how it makes you feel (the latter is hard to argue against, though keep it brief). For example: 'Laura, what you have just done is not how we expect students to behave in this classroom. It makes me feel upset that you would talk to me in this way and damage the learning of the class. I would not talk to you like that and I think you have the ability to behave more positively.' Here we are seeking to defuse tension and make the student reflect on the consequences of their actions, as well the alternative choice they could have made. If the behaviour persists, the student will need to face a sanction such as being asked to leave the room. If it stops, you should still follow up by talking to the student about what happened and what led them to behave like this.

Solution 2: Sometimes students can challenge your authority in a way that is hard to deal with then and there. For example, you might be more concerned with the learning of the remainder of the class than devoting your energy to dealing with a student who is making snide remarks. In this situation, make a mental note of the behaviour and ask the student to stay behind at the end of the lesson. Talk to them about how they acted, making it clear that you observed what they did and are unhappy about it. Tell them that you do not expect it to happen again and that, if it does, you will escalate the situation by informing a relevant senior member of staff such as a head of year or team leader.

Solution 3: On occasion, a student's challenge to your authority may be so severe that you have no choice but to go directly to the application of a sanction, bypassing the process of seeking behaviour change. For example, a student may come into your lesson late, ignore you, and start shouting across the room to their friend. In these situations, it is good to apply the sanction immediately, so as to stress the unacceptability of the behaviour, but to remain calm as you do this. The temptation can be to react emotionally because of the surprise and severity of the behaviour. You may decide that the situation warrants an emotional response, of course. But make this a decision rather than a reaction – you can then control it and use it as a means through which to stress disapprobation. After the sanction has been applied, ask yourself why the student acted in this way – they are unlikely to have done it for no reason. When you go to speak to the student, disarm them by starting with the following: 'I'm really surprised you would behave towards me like that. I'm worried that something must have happened to cause this – can you tell me where your behaviour has come from?' This undermines the student's expectations (they will probably be ready for a verbally bruising encounter) and makes it clear that, while you will pull them up on poor behaviour, your primary aim remains, at all times, to help and support them.

Ignoring Instructions

Explanation: One or more students ignore your instructions. This could be deliberate or unintentional.

Solution 1: Ascertain why students have ignored your instructions. Ask them if they understand what you want them to do. Ask if they need you to re-explain the request you are making. If they require additional support or more information, provide it. If they do not, ask them to do what you have requested. This process is hard to argue against because it is predicated on you demonstrating your interest in supporting students. Few students will want to persist in not following your instructions if you have just spelt out different ways in which you want to support them.

Solution 2: Praise the example of students who have followed your instructions. Do this conspicuously, verbalising the link between the students' decisions and the learning they are doing as a result. Draw the attention of those who are not following instructions with a line such as: 'Marcus, that's what I want to see, thanks, just like Donna and Hayley. They're focussed on their learning.' Here, we are giving the student a model to imitate. This removes the possible excuse that they do not understand your instructions and offers vicarious reinforcement of positive behaviour.

Solution 3: If only a few students are not following your instructions and you feel this runs contrary to the behaviour you are used to seeing and expecting in your classroom, ask them to come to the front of the room to speak to you. When they arrive, point out that the rest of the class are engaged in their learning and making positive decisions to work hard.

Explain that you do not expect them to continue with behaviour that stops them learning. Ask if they need any of the instructions re-explaining. If they do, provide this. If they don't, ask them to return to their seats and to make a positive choice to apply themselves.

Rudeness

Explanation: A student is rude to you through their attitude, behaviour or language. This usually happens in front of other students.

Solution 1: Call out the behaviour immediately. Rudeness often continues – or gets worse – if you don't do this. The implicit message in not dealing with such behaviour straightaway is that it is in some way acceptable and can be repeated by the student or students in question. Draw attention to the fact that the behaviour is rude and, if necessary, state why this is so (some students can be rude without realising it). Indicate that you do not expect such behaviour to be repeated. At this point, you may want to convey what sanction will follow if the student doesn't meet your expectations; this will depend on your reading of the situation (a reprimand of the student's behaviour is often enough to elicit a positive change).

Solution 2: Remind the student or students in question of your expectations and the norms and values which underpin your classroom culture. Ask them to explain whether or not their rudeness fits with these. Clearly it does not. In most situations, student will acknowledge this and accept the implicit rebuke. If they do not, explain why they ought to, then give them the opportunity to change their behaviour. If they do this, fantastic. If they do not, escalate the situation by applying a sanction.

Solution 3: Couch your response in terms of reciprocity and respect. Highlight the fact that behaviour is communication and that the communication you give out mirrors the communication you want to receive. Indicate to the student in question that you do not treat them rudely and that, as a result, you do not expect them to treat you rudely either. Press home the point that they come into the classroom expecting a level of civility and respect but that this will be undermined or undeserved if they continue to behave in a way which is rude. Give students a choice to make a positive change. If they do not, apply a sanction and explain that this is a direct consequence of the rudeness they are displaying. Finally, give them the opportunity to apologise and to change their behaviour – let them know what they need to do to make the matter right.

Persistent Lateness

Explanation: One or more students are persistently late to your class.

Solution 1: Explain to the whole class why lateness is a problem and what sanctions you will apply to students who are late. Make clear what your expectations are and indicate what circumstances represent an acceptable reason for not meeting these (being held back by another teacher, transport problems on the way to school). Enforce your sanctions rigorously over the coming weeks – to those who are persistently late and to those who are late as a one-off. Punctuality will quickly increase as a result.

Solution 2: Arguably, lateness is a whole-school issue as well as an issue for individual teachers. This does not mean we should disown responsibility for dealing with it, but that we might consider invoking the support of wider school structures straightaway. If a student is late, ask them why. Should no good reason be forthcoming, indicate the sanction that will apply and contact the member of the pastoral team responsible for their welfare. Ask them to join you in applying a sanction and communicating high expectations to the student in question. Ensure all sanctions are followed up and accompanied by a clear explanation of why lateness is unacceptable.

Solution 3: Some students struggle to be punctual. These students may be persistently late, not because they are being deliberately tardy, but because they do not have the skills and strategies to keep to time. In these situations, you should teach students how to avoid lateness. Basic strategies such as aiming to arrive before the lesson starts rather than when it starts, wearing a watch and planning what time to leave the playground can all be a new experience for underprepared students.

Checking to see whether latecomers lack such tools will give you the chance to pass on these approaches as and when appropriate.

Disengagement

Explanation: A student disengages from the lesson. This usually takes the form of passivity and/or apathy and tends to see the student withdrawing physically and psychologically from the learning.

Solution 1: Take the student aside and ask them why they are disengaged. Use probing questions to find out if they have specific issues with the subject, topic or learning environment. Sometimes these can be dealt with, sometimes the student will have to learn to put up with them. Acting in this way will give you access to information you can use to help re-engage the student in question. It will also demonstrate that you are interested in their thoughts and that you want to help them. This builds rapport and, in some cases, is actually what disengaged behaviour is fundamentally about – gaining a little of the teacher's attention.

Solution 2: Pair the student with a supportive or enthusiastic peer. This could involve an alteration to your seating plan or the inclusion of paired tasks in which you provide guidance on every pairing in the class (subtly including this particular one on the list!). While the disengaged student is working with their peer, observe them to see if the decision has had an effect. If it has, leave things be. If it has not, intervene to encourage the student to work positively with their peer. This sees you invoking the underlying expectations of social interaction and using these to alter the disengaged student's behaviour.

Solution 3: Stress to the student in question that your expectations include learners retaining focus through the course of the entire lesson. Tie this to the wider aim of your lessons – to promote learning and maximise progress. If possible, connect this to the student's goals as well. Offer an opportunity for them to explain why they are choosing to disengage. If nothing is forthcoming, direct their attention back to your expectations and the task in hand. If they do indicate a cause, address it and then re-direct them onto the task.

Whole-Class Noise Levels

Explanation: The class as a whole are too noisy, will not fall to silence or do not heed your instructions about how much noise is permissible.

Solution 1: Plan lessons which do not give students the opportunity to make noise. This means removing group work and discussion activities. On doing this, explain to students what is happening and indicate that the noise levels in the class do not meet your expectations. Explain that, if students can display a positive attitude over the next few lessons, you will gradually reintroduce group work and discussion. This ties the future of the lessons to the choices students make as well as the effort and hard work they exhibit.

Solution 2: Create a means through which to specify noise levels. For example, you might develop a five point scale running from silent to loud. You would then explain this to students, giving them a chance to gain a sense of what each level sounds like. When introducing activities, bring out the scale and tell students what level of noise is appropriate for the task. If noise levels go too high, gather the students' attention, refer them to the scale and ask them change their behaviour. This is an excellent way through which to help students understand the amount of noise they create and what your expectations mean in tangible terms.

Solution 3: When you want students to be quiet, count down from five to one. Then, wait for silence. Get students into the habit of expecting this and responding to it swiftly. Praise students who follow the instructions and remind students who do not that they need to come on board. Developing a technique like this allows you to control the noise levels in your classroom very effectively – it is a tool to which you can return again and again.

Class Dynamics

Explanation: The relationships and interactions within your class are in some way detrimental to learning. They might give rise to negative interactions, an atmosphere of discomfort or they might lead to students who are not focussed on the learning becoming dominant voices.

Solution 1: Rearrange the seating plan. This is the simplest, most common fall-back position. Dynamics are heavily affected by who students can see, influence and talk to. If you observe the dynamics of the class working against a positive, learning-focussed atmosphere, examine the seating plan and identify the changes you could make to improve matters. When students next come to your classroom, display the new seating plan on the board and firmly insist that students follow it. For maximum effect, present the plan as a fait accompli, rather than as open for negotiation.

Solution 2: Consider changing the layout of your room. If students are sat in groups, perhaps they would be better in rows? If they are in rows, maybe a horseshoe would work better? Looking at the consequences of how the room is laid out will help you to decide whether changing this could have a positive impact. As a rule, rows facing the front is the layout in which the teacher is able to exert the most control over students – good if you have a particularly lively class who struggle to stick to your expectations in the face of the prevailing dynamic.

Solution 3: Plan your lessons so they militate against the dynamic. If the class tend to play off each other to the point at which learning breaks down, minimise opportunities for group interaction. Similarly, if students who are not particularly learning-focussed have become the dominant voices, plan group work tasks in which they are spread through the room and find themselves outnumbered in each group by students who are focussed on their learning.

Class Clown

Explanation: An individual student seeks status by taking on the role of class clown. This student focuses their attention on playing up to this role rather than engaging with the learning.

Solution 1: Give the student in question another way to gain status. This could involve assigning them responsibility for something such as handing out the books or identifying who makes the most interesting or perceptive comment during the course of a discussion. Another option is to give that student one-to-one support about their learning. This helps them to gain status through making progress, diminishing the reward they receive, psychologically, from playing the role of clown.

Solution 2: Draw a firm distinction for the student in question between when humour is acceptable and when it is not. Stress that it is not acceptable when it interferes with the learning, causing the student or their peers to fall below your expectations. Doing this gives the student license to have some fun in class – which, in many cases, may actually help them to work better. At the same time, however, it teaches them that they must prioritise learning above having fun and that the latter must always be subjugated to the demands of the former.

Solution 3: Ask the student to stay behind after the lesson. Explain what you have observed about their behaviour. Indicate why being able to make people laugh is often a good thing and praise the effort they are able to exert in achieving this end. Then, ask them whether the classroom is the place to pursue such a goal and why they are not prepared to channel their substantial efforts into creating work of a high standard. Ask them whether they have considered developing their comedy in their own time and make a clear distinction between this as a leisure activity and what you expect from them in lessons. This approach demonstrates that you have a sense of humour and admire the student's ability to draw laughter while at the same time teaching them that there needs to be a clear delineation regarding when such behaviour is appropriate and when it isn't.

Fixed Mindsets

Explanation: Students show a reluctance to challenge themselves or exert effort, believing that both these behaviours are fruitless because intelligence is ultimately a fixed, innate quality.

Solution 1: Praise the processes in which students engage, particularly effort. Every student can try, regardless of where they are at with their learning. Convey this message and reinforce it. This breaks down the view in students' minds that effort does not bring reward. It does so by positively reinforcing the application of effort, turning it into a norm which is worthy of pursuit.

Solution 2: Use examples to demonstrate to students why and how intelligence can be changed. An easy one is to ask students to explain to you what they knew and understood a year ago compared to what they know and understand now. From here, you can ask them to explain why their intelligence has grown before making the link (if they don't make it themselves) between the effort they have exerted and the changes which have been wrought. Another option is to draw students' attention to some basic brain physiognomy, illustrating for them the fact that our neuronal networks are plastic and malleable, that they can change over time and that the ways in which we use our minds and the effort we put in has a significant impact on this.

Solution 3: Make embracing challenge and learning from mistakes a norm in your classroom. Ask students to tell you when the work is too easy and apologise to them when it is, offering to provide a harder, more challenging alternative. Watch your language so as to ensure you do not inadvertently punish or chastise mistakes, instead reconceptualising them as learning opportunities – particularly in the context of trial and error.

Social Chat

Explanation: Pairs, small group of students or the whole class are inclined to engage in social conversation unconnected to the learning. They may protest that this has no impact 'because they are still doing work,' or they may make no pretence to justify their behaviour.

Solution 1: Directly address the contention that social chat is acceptable if it accompanies students doing work. To do this, ask students to reflect on the main aim of your lesson and to contrast this with the aims of break and lunchtime. The point here is to draw a firmer distinction in students' minds between the different aspects of the school day. Plenty of time is provided during which students can talk among themselves about whatever they please. The corollary of this is that there is no excuse for using up energy and focus in lessons when this could be more productively directed towards the learning.

Solution 2: Play up your expectations. For example, if a group of students are engaged in social chat while they are working on the main activity, go over to them and ask how they are getting on with the extension task. When they tell you they have not yet reached it, explain that you are surprised. You assumed they must be stretching their thinking because they have the time to divide their focus between the learning and other matters. Indicate that you are disappointed and would like to see all of them on the extension task in the next ten minutes (or whatever timescale is appropriate). This technique reacquaints students with your expectations and reminds them of the link between actions and consequences (the consequence here being your disapprobation).

Solution 3: Use your seating plan to separate friendship groups and to ensure that students sit near peers with whom they are unlikely to discuss unrelated matters. This requires you to know at least a little bit about your class and so may not be achievable at first. A couple of weeks into the new school year, however, and you should have a pretty good idea of any changes you need to make.

In terms of a summary, let me conclude this analysis of how to solve the various problems and scenarios by providing an outline of the key points common to all of the above:

- To deal effectively with any behaviour issue you must be proactive and decisive.

- Base your decisions on an analysis of what is happening and why you believe it to be happening.

- Be aware that multiple solutions can be found to most problems and that part of becoming better at behaviour management involves trying things out, seeing what works and what doesn't, and then using this information to make improved decisions in the future.

- When you act, remain positive and assertive, remind students of your expectations and give them a choice.

- Do not expect all problems to disappear straightaway. On many occasions you will need to keep applying your solution over time in order to habituate students into a new way of acting. Be persistent!

Chapter Ten – Collected Chapter Summaries

Here I have collected together the summaries from each of the previous chapters. This gives you an easy-to-use reference tool to which you can refer when necessary.

Chapter One – What is Behaviour?

- Behaviour refers to our external actions – it includes the things we do and say.

- Behaviour is caused. These causes can be internal, external or a combination of both.

- Behaviour communicates messages. Some of these are clear, some ambiguous. Some intended, some not. Some known by the individual whose behaviour we observe, some not.

- All messages are interpreted. Interpretations may differ from what was intended.

- Much behaviour stems from motives, with these being rooted in reason, emotion and sentiments.

- Children and young adults are learning. Their development includes learning about behaviour – every teacher is a teacher of more than just the curriculum

- The behaviour of children and young adults is malleable and open to change.

Chapter Two – Norms, Values, Roles and Status

- Culture is made up of norms, values, roles and status.

- Your classroom culture rests on what you define for each of these.

- Having defined what you want your classroom culture to be, you should communicate this clearly and consistently.

- Demonstrating high expectations at all times is an excellent way to do this. It should be the cornerstone of your behaviour management.

- Specifying the constituents of your classroom culture places you in a stronger position from which to communicate these. This, in turn, makes it easier for students to meet and exceed your expectations.

Chapter Three – Rules, Boundaries and Consistency

- Rules need to be defined and communicated.

- Your rules should reflect the culture you want to create and should be applied fairly.

- Boundaries should be defined and communicated.

- Your boundaries should be tied to your rules and carefully policed.

- Sanctions should be defined and communicated.

- Your sanctions should be applied fairly and carefully and should always be followed through.

- Consistency in all the above is the key to training your students in good habits.

Chapter Four – Planning for Learning

- The lessons you plan have a major impact on student behaviour.

- Bearing this in mind allows you to plan more effectively.

- Ensuring students are able to experience success and that they have their thinking suitably challenge is always helpful.

- Understanding how students are likely to experience your lessons gives you a chance to make important changes in advance of teaching them.

- Thoughtful preparation and good organisation go a long way to helping you manage behaviour effectively.

- The information you elicit when you teach your lessons (how students respond, how they engage with the learning, how they deal with certain activities and so forth) is information you can use to inform any subsequent planning. This allows you to improve the quality of what you do, resulting in lesson plans which are increasingly effective in terms of how they help you to manage behaviour.

Chapter Five – Using Praise

- Look for opportunities to praise students you teach, including those students who may otherwise get overlooked.

- Deliver genuine, specific praise which focusses on processes and efforts.

- Make use of verbal, written and non-verbal praise.

- Use praise to reinforce the positive behaviours you want to see – this includes through vicarious reinforcement (where students see other students receiving praise).

- Use praise as a reward to acknowledge the effort and work individuals, groups and the whole-class have put into your lessons and activities.

- Remember that praise is a means through which status can be achieved and acknowledged. Take this into account when looking for opportunities to deliver praise.

- Giving praise does not have to be confined to the classroom. Look for other ways in which you can use praise to build rapport, support your students and help them to achieve highly.

Chapter Six – Eliminating Low-Level Disruption

- Reconceptualise low-level disruption as unacceptable.

- Communicate this message to your students by stressing and reinforcing your high expectations.

- Look for low-level disruption and challenge it as soon as you see it. Do so positively and assertively, giving students the opportunity to choose how they will improve their behaviour.

- Identify, define and apply sanctions where appropriate.

- Empower and engage students so that low-level disruption becomes a less attractive option.

- Modify your language so that it supports your wider aims of securing good behaviour.

- Praise and reward good behaviour, including focussing on the work and choosing to change from negative to positive actions.

Chapter Seven – Creating Engagement

- Engagement is motivational. It gives students purpose and nearly always leads to better behaviour.

- Disengaged students tend to withdraw from learning physically and psychologically. They may also look to gain status within the classroom through other means.

- If you make creating engagement a focus of your planning and teaching you are likely to stimulate excellent behaviour.

- Engagement can be encouraged by contextualising learning, either in relation to the real-world or to prior experience.

- Ensuring all students are sufficiently challenged and finding ways to help students to be successful is also good.

- As is the creation and communication of joint goals.

- Finally, you can help students to learn actively by ensuring your lessons do not allow them to remain passive; variety is one route to achieving this, as is stimulating student endeavour by helping them to visualise the progress they have made.

Chapter Eight – Building Rapport

- Good rapport means having harmonious, positive relationships with your students in which you and they are working towards a shared goal and with a shared understanding.

- Rapport matters because it helps foster a focussed learning environment, makes behaviour management easier and significantly increases the chance that lessons will be successful, that students will learn more and that this learning will be enjoyable.

- Every aspect of your communication conveys messages which can support or work against your attempts to build rapport.

- Treating students as individuals, demonstrating that you think they are important and making it clear that you have an interest in their ideas, wellbeing and success will help you to establish rapport.

- Any strategy you use to try to build rapport will be far more effective if it is underpinned by a genuine desire to establish and maintain good relationships.

Chapter Nine – Problems and Scenarios

- To deal effectively with any behaviour issue you must be proactive and decisive.

- Base your decisions on an analysis of what is happening and why you believe it to be happening.

- Be aware that multiple solutions can be found to most problems and that part of becoming better at behaviour management involves trying things out, seeing what works and what doesn't, and then using this information to make improved decisions in the future.

- When you act, remain positive and assertive, remind students of your expectations and give them a choice.

- Do not expect all problems to disappear straightaway. On many occasions you will need to keep applying your solution over time in order to habituate students into a new way of acting. Be persistent!

Conclusion

We conclude with just a few brief words, reminding us of those first set out in the introduction.

The children and young adults with whom we work are learning all the time. This learning extends beyond the formal curriculum to include things such as behaviour, manners, morals and the unwritten rules of society.

Behaviour can be learned. All of us can change and grow.

Through the way in which you teach, the lessons you plan, the expectations you communicate, the choices you outline, the sanctions you apply, the explanations you give, the engagement you create, the praise you provide and the consistency you demonstrate, you will be able to shape the behaviour of your students so that it is positive, effortful and focussed on learning.

This will not always be easy – in fact, at times, it will be tough.

But by remaining set on your goal, persisting and acknowledging that we all learn when faced with challenges and difficulties, you will be well-placed to secure improvements over time. And as these improvements add up, you will see and feel change taking place in front of you. And you will know that the hard work was worth it!

So good luck on your journey to excellent behaviour management. I hope it proves fruitful – for you and for your students.

Select Bibliography

The following books are worth a look; all can be purchased via Amazon:

Phil Beadle and John Murphy, *Why are you shouting at us?: The dos and don'ts of behaviour management*

Tom Bennett, *The Behaviour Guru: Behaviour Management Solutions for Teachers*

Mary Cay Ricci, *Mindsets in the Classroom: Building a Culture of Success and Student Achievement in Schools*

Sue Cowley, *The Seven C's of Positive Behaviour Management*

Simon Ellis and Janet Tod, *Behaviour for Learning: Proactive Approaches to Behaviour Management*

Peter Hook and Andy Vass, *Behaviour Management Pocketbook*

Molly Potter, *100 Ideas for Primary Teachers: Behaviour Management*

Bill Rogers, *Classroom Behaviour*

Bill Rogers, *Cracking the Hard Class*

Bill Rogers, *How to Manage Children's Challenging Behaviour*

The TES website also has lots of excellent resources, advice and support around behaviour:

www.tes.co.uk

www.tes.co.uk/behaviour

Printed in Great Britain
by Amazon.co.uk, Ltd.,
Marston Gate.